USING FOCUS GROUPS TO LISTEN, LEARN, AND
LEAD IN HIGHER EDUCATION

USING FOCUS GROUPS TO LISTEN, LEARN, AND LEAD IN HIGHER EDUCATION

Mona J. E. Danner, J. Worth Pickering, and Tisha M. Paredes

Foreword by Jillian Kinzie

Sty/us

STERLING, VIRGINIA

Published by Stylus Publishing, LLC.
22883 Quicksilver Drive
Sterling, Virginia 20166-2019

Library of Congress Cataloging-in-Publication Data
Names: Danner, Mona J. E., author. | Pickering, James Worth, author. |
    Paredes, Tisha M., author.
Title: Using focus groups to listen, learn, and lead in higher education /
    Mona J.E. Danner, J. Worth Pickering, and Tisha M. Paredes.
Description: First edition. |
Sterling, Virginia : Stylus Publishing, LLC, [2018] |
Includes bibliographical references and index.
Identifiers: LCCN 2017034873 (print) |
LCCN 2017055535 (ebook) |
ISBN 9781620365984 (uPDF) |
ISBN 9781620365991 (mobi, uPDF) |
ISBN 9781620365960 (cloth : acid free paper) |
ISBN 9781620365977 (pbk. : acid free paper) |
ISBN 9781620365984 (library networkable e-edition) |
ISBN 9781620365991 (consumer e-edition)
Subjects: LCSH: Education, Higher--Research--Methodology. |
Universities and colleges--Administration--Decision making. |
Focus groups.
Classification: LCC LB2326.3 (ebook) |
LCC LB2326.3 .D36 2018 (print) |
DDC 378.007--dc23
LC record available at https://lccn.loc.gov/2017034873

13-digit ISBN: 978-1-62036-596-0 (cloth)
13-digit ISBN: 978-1-62036-597-7 (paperback)
13-digit ISBN: 978-1-62036-598-4 (library networkable e-edition)
13-digit ISBN: 978-1-62036-599-1 (consumer e-edition)

Printed in the United States of America

All first editions printed on acid-free paper
that meets the American National Standards Institute
Z39-48 Standard.

Bulk Purchases

Quantity discounts are available for use in workshops and for
staff development.
Call 1-800-232-0223

First Edition, 2018

CONTENTS

FOREWORD

Expectations for the use of evidence to guide decision-making, assess effectiveness, and demonstrate impact in colleges and universities is high. Although much of the current fascination is with accessing "big data" and using rigorous data modeling to reveal obstacles to student success, there is tremendous value in integrating evidence from a variety of sources to satisfy accountability demands in higher education.

My work with the National Survey of Student Engagement (NSSE), a project that assesses educational quality in higher education through surveys of students and faculty, has made me a strong proponent of survey data. Customized survey reports provide institutions reliable peer comparison results and statistically significant differences. However, every year I marvel at the substantive information generated from an open-ended comment prompt at the end of the survey. Students are invited to respond to an institutionally chosen prompt, including: "What one change would you most like to see implemented that would improve the educational experience at this institution, and what one thing should not be changed?" or "Please describe the most significant learning experience you have had so far at this institution". These prompts elicit substantive insights about educational experiences that matter to students. For example, some students write paragraphs describing a professor who offered vital advice or the significance of their involvement in a club or organization. In 2017, one NSSE participating institution had more than 2,200 individual student responses! Students say they appreciate the occasion to express their opinions freely about their college experience.

Qualitative approaches to assessment, such as student responses to well-designed prompts, and interviews and focus groups, provide useful information about institutional effectiveness. In fact, they offer deeper understandings of social phenomenon than could ever be obtained from purely quantitative methods. Conducting focus groups is a key approach to solicit a wider range of perspectives on campus practices and gauge participants' commitments to their views. For example, if NSSE results do not comport with what a campus believes about itself, I encourage the use of focus groups as a way to invite students to collectively interpret a finding and/or provide detailed examples of their experiences. Asking students for their input and specific instances of their experiences with services can provide critical insights into undergraduate education. In these situations, focus groups generate explicit illustrations and rich understandings of students' experiences. Even more, when conducted with respect for students' views, can simultaneously foster students' investment in the institution and perception that the institution cares.

Qualitative methods are particularly conducive to studying the college context. Because students are already interacting in groups, including in classes, athletic teams, student organizations, and residence hall communities, focus groups can seem like a natural extension of this interaction. In addition, as the authors of *Using Focus Groups to Listen, Learn, and Lead in Higher Education* point out, universities are rich in terms of people with the listening, questioning, moderating, and reporting skills necessary for conducting qualitative research. Yet, some development is still necessary to optimize these skills and to efficiently implement focus groups. This book provides interested campus educators and researchers a tested, accessible approach to collecting data via focus groups.

In the chapters that follow, Mona J. E. Danner, J. Worth Pickering, and Tisha M. Paredes generously share their expert knowledge, practical advice, detailed logistical information, and facilitation techniques for conducting focus groups. As someone who has conducted many focus groups to learn about students' experiences and has encouraged other campus educators and researchers to employ these approaches, I appreciate the technical expertise outlined in this book. Although readers seeking a how-to resource might be inclined to head directly to the succinct methods chapters and the appendices filled with sample protocols, useful guides, and adaptable invitations and templates, it would be a serious oversight to by-pass the important early chapters that set the context and emphasize the important first step of defining the purpose of focus groups and developing appropriate research questions. Practical chapters on setting up and moderating focus groups as well as essential details for reporting results provide readers solid grounding in focus group methods. The final chapter offers a helpful cautionary tale about focus groups, discussing what can go awry and introducing the realities of college and university work that can derail or present obstacles to even the best laid plans.

Focus groups can be an effective and efficient qualitative method for practitioners, researchers, and students studying higher education and the college environment. As expectations for accountability and evidence-based decision in higher education grow, more institutions need to ensure that a range of approaches are employed to collect data about educational quality. *Using Focus Groups to Listen, Learn, and Lead in Higher Education* is a perfect resource for increasing our repertoire.

Jillian Kinzie
Indiana University Bloomington

PREFACE

This book describes the application of focus groups, a qualitative methodology, in institutions of higher education within the context of increasing calls for data to address the big questions of access, affordability, and accountability. The book makes the case that relying on metrics and quantitative data alone to explore these questions is insufficient. Quantitative data and metrics often identify or describe concerns and problems in higher education but rarely offer solutions and improvements, precisely because they lack student and faculty voices. While surveys and interviews attempt to address this, the former lack nuance and the latter are expensive and time-consuming. Focus groups emerge as a rigorous and relevant qualitative research tool that is cost-effective when conducted using the method described in this book.

Focus groups are confidential group discussions with a trained and skilled moderator using open-ended questions that promote interaction in order to explore participants' perspectives and experiences in a structured but relaxed atmosphere. Designed to generate rigorous qualitative data, focus groups allow the opportunity to listen, learn, and lead; that is, they allow leaders to listen to and learn from the very people who will be affected by whatever changes are under consideration. While informing decision-making, focus groups also build community and increase participants' sense of value and commitment to the institution because they involve stakeholders in helping to shape policies and practices.

Paying professional researchers to collect qualitative data is inefficient and wasteful because they are expensive outsiders who still require significant in-house assistance. The economic challenges faced by institutions of higher education, especially those in the public sector, mean that few funds exist to support such endeavors. Fortunately, universities are uniquely resource-rich environments in terms of the skills necessary for conducting qualitative research. Universities are filled with people who know how to listen, ask questions, take notes, write reports, and make presentations; after all, every faculty member and administrator and many staff have been college students, and they continue to use these very skills in their work. Most importantly, they understand the context, language, and nuances of their institution.

Using Focus Groups to Listen, Learn, and Lead in Higher Education provides a single resource that details a proven and rigorous methodology that helps readers understand and learn why, when, and how to use focus groups in colleges and universities. Written particularly for upper-level administrators and institutional research and assessment staff, this book will also be a valuable resource for college deans, department and program chairs and directors, and faculty leaders, as well as administrative unit directors including those in auxiliary and student services, alumni associations, and university foundations. Faculty teaching and students enrolled in higher education administration and leadership programs will find it useful as they consider how to respond to today's data demands.

The Old Dominion University (ODU) Team has developed a methodology to use focus groups to collect, analyze, and confirm data to listen, learn, and lead in higher education and now offers it to you. Readers will learn

- how focus groups inform the other qualitative and quantitative data collected,
- the many ways that focus groups can be applied in a variety of higher education settings to collect a wide range of information,
- that focus groups are a theoretically rigorous and empirically relevant method to gather qualitative data for evidence-based decision-making, and
- exactly when to use and how to conduct focus groups.

The authors are uniquely positioned to help readers in this process. The ODU Team has conducted focus groups with many campus, nonprofit, local, and international community organizations to assist them in assessing student learning, transition, and preparedness for the workforce, as well as evaluating organizations' work and planning future projects. Since 1990, the ODU Team has conducted more than 100 focus groups to learn more about

- what the university is, what it should be, and how to get there as perceived by the senior leadership team, faculty, staff, and students;
- the strengths, weaknesses, opportunities, and threats (SWOT), for strategic planning purposes, as perceived by faculty, administrators, and staff;
- the experiences, needs, and problems of first-year and transfer students;
- the perceptions of employers of students' abilities and success on the job;

- how graduate program administrators do their jobs and what they need from other units;
- how external constituencies view the university and what kinds of things might attract them to campus;
- how students view the impact of a new, multidisciplinary general education course for all first-year students;
- why students attend an international university for their training and stay to work in the local community;
- how well an organization is serving its community and in what directions the organization should go;
- how an administrative area serves the research and teaching activities of faculty and doctoral students;
- how staff perceive the university community experience and the improvements needed; and
- some possible topics, feedback on the topic selected, and the implementation plan for the university's Quality Enhancement Plan required by the Southern Association of Colleges and Schools Commission on Colleges (SACSCOC), the regional accreditor.

The ODU Team has also conducted focus group training and taught the ODU Method at workshops for the American College Personnel Association (ACPA), the Southern Association for College Student Affairs (SACSA), the Virginia Assessment Group (VAG), SACSCOC, and Pontificia Universidad Católica Madre y Maestra (Pucamyma) in the Dominican Republic. The ODU Method to collect, analyze, and validate the data gathered from focus groups works for teaching and administrative faculty, staff, undergraduate and graduate students, alumni, employers, and community members. The totality of these experiences has allowed us to validate the ODU Method in institutions of higher education and nonprofit community organizations. Participants consistently praise the workshops and have reported back to us their use of the ODU Method and the high value of the method's consistency and accuracy.

Using Focus Groups to Listen, Learn, and Lead in Higher Education provides all of the practical information needed to help your institution conduct focus groups using the ODU Method, whatever your experience level with focus groups, from none to some experience as either a focus group participant or a focus group moderator. The book also offers important resources to those who have led focus group projects and want to improve their process and make their focus groups both more relevant and more rigorous.

The following chapters provide readers with practical guidance using concrete examples that will allow them to:

- design and defend a focus group project with consideration of basic qualitative data methodology and analysis principles;
- determine when focus groups are appropriate or not;
- develop a Research Proposal with a purpose statement and research questions;
- write focus group questions;
- design an effective Moderator's Guide;
- select, recruit, and train moderators;
- identify and recruit focus group participants;
- manage the logistics for conducting focus groups; and
- analyze focus group data and draft an accurate report.

Two Notes on Language

Because research, like life, can be complex and because exact specificity in both writing and reading can be tiring, we use two linguistic shortcuts throughout the book. *Universities, colleges,* and *institutions of higher education* are used interchangeably to refer to legally authorized and accredited institutions offering postsecondary academic or vocational training or credit leading to a certificate or degree. Readers should assume that each term is meant to be inclusive and that a particular choice is made only for writing and reading stylistic purposes. *The ODU Team, the Research Team,* or simply *the Team* refers to those who design and direct focus groups to listen, learn, and lead, whether at ODU or the reader's own institution.

ACKNOWLEDGMENTS

Special thanks to James A. Calliotte and Stephen C. Zerwas, our early colleagues who helped lay the groundwork for the ODU Method of conducting focus groups. We also appreciate the many clients, moderators, and participants with whom we have worked over the decades who challenged us in ways that led to important refinements.

EXPLORING THE BIG QUESTIONS IN HIGHER EDUCATION

Access, Affordability, Accountability

The desirability of a college education is well established. Nearly 20 million people were enrolled in college in 2012, and almost 32% of American adults have earned at least a bachelor's degree, which was up from 5% in 1940 (U.S. Census Bureau, 2013, 2016). Possessing a college degree is associated with higher initial wages, lifetime earnings, retirement income, and overall wealth (Bureau of Labor Statistics, 2016; Julian, 2012; Julian & Kominski, 2011). Those with a college degree also report better health and happiness, a sense of optimism, and more opportunities (Cutler & Lleras-Muney, 2012; Egerter, Braveman, Sadegh-Nobari, Grossman-Kahn, & Dekker, 2009; Pew Research Center, 2014). Indeed, a college education is key to the American Dream, as people rightly see college as bringing increased opportunities to themselves and their children (Constable & Clement, 2014; Immerwahr & Johnson, 2010). Businesses seek college-educated employees for their critical thinking and communication skills. Society as a whole and democracy in particular benefit from an educated citizenry and electorate.

It is precisely because a college education is so important that questions about higher education abound in the United States today. The big questions concern access, affordability, and accountability (Conner & Rabovsky, 2011). "Who gets a college education?"—access—depends on who applies, is admitted, and enrolls. "How much does college cost?"—affordability—centers on the price tag as well as who pays and how. "Does college deliver on its promises?"—accountability—is often captured by outcomes such as how many

1

students stay enrolled (retention and persistence), graduate on time, get jobs in their field, or apply for advanced degrees, and their starting salaries.

Dramatic increases in tuition and alarming stories about student loan debt likely drive the biggest of the big questions in higher education today: "Does college deliver on its promises?" that is, "Is higher education giving us (as individual students and graduates, taxpayers, and society) the best value for our money?" At the same time, college has come to be seen as a private good primarily benefiting the one earning the degree, and so the individual should foot more of the bill for an education. These concerns have collided with growing distrust in public institutions to generate attacks on colleges and universities. Pandering politicians and media pundits have criticized higher education for promoting "unnecessary and worthless" degrees such as those in the arts and humanities and containing scientists who know nothing about their fields of study; professors derided as lazy, liberal, or caring for research over teaching; and administrative bloat and Taj Mahal–like amenities (Belkin & Thurm, 2012; Jaschik, 2012; Kiley, 2013; Martin, 2012; "The 13 Most Useless Majors," 2012).

The increased demands for accountability and oversight from politicians, taxpayers, parents, and students require more and better data for evidence-based decision-making at all levels and across all campus units. Colleges and universities are awash in *quantitative* data, as everything is counted: from student admissions to graduation rates, and enrollment to suspension, not to mention all manner of evaluations including test scores, grades, and assessment, and the plethora of employment numbers related to faculty, administrators, and staff. Indeed, "'accountability' is the watchword—everything that can be counted is counted, and everything that cannot be counted doesn't count" (Rawlings, 2014). While all of these data provide important information about *frequencies*, the actual experiences of stakeholders are less clear as these data tell us nothing about the *meanings* behind the numbers. The reality is that "not everything that can be counted counts, and not everything that counts can be counted" (Cameron, 1963, p. 13). Satisfaction and opinion surveys provide some insight, but they rarely uncover the complexity of experiences, reasons, and feelings that contextualize the judgments proffered. Anecdotes add depth and bring some understanding, but individual stories are neither representative nor generalizable. It is *qualitative* data that can provide the context to understand the massive amounts of quantitative data collected in higher education environments. Qualitative methods allow users to address the elusive "Why?" question in order to further the understanding of *what really counts*. Together the data derived from both quantitative and qualitative methodologies help us explore the big questions in higher education.

Exploring the Big Questions With Quantitative and Qualitative Methods and Data

All of the big questions surrounding access, affordability, and accountability are answerable using quantitative or qualitative data, depending on the research question. In the latest edition of his widely used book *Research Design*, Creswell (2014) succinctly defined *qualitative, quantitative,* and *mixed methods* research strategies. On one end of the continuum is *qualitative research*, which Creswell defined as "an approach for exploring and understanding the meaning individuals or groups ascribe to a social or human problems [*sic*]" (p. 4). And on the other end of the continuum, Creswell defined *quantitative research* as "an approach for testing objective theories by examining the relationship among variables" (p. 4). Incorporating aspects of both qualitative and quantitative approaches, *mixed methods* is defined as "an approach to inquiry involving collecting both quantitative and qualitative data, integrating the two forms of data, and using distinct designs that may involve philosophical assumptions and theoretical frameworks" (Creswell, 2014, p. 4). All three research strategies are valuable, and the choice of one over the others depends on the research question posed. In this book, we argue for the value of the qualitative data obtained from a rigorous and relevant focus group methodology to answer questions of great depth and provide deep meaning to quantitative data.

Whether to take a quantitative or qualitative approach to various issues depends on the research question and one's orientation to, or preference for, collecting data, as well as the orientation of the person or group asking the questions. A mixed methods approach that uses both quantitative and qualitative data often enhances the answers (Creswell, 2014). For example, many of the big questions in higher education today are initially, and superficially, addressed via a number of established "metrics" or counts; additional quantitative data can be obtained with surveys of the appropriate populations. But if we want to truly understand the experiences of those affected by access, affordability, and accountability, we must listen to them and hear their voices, and that requires qualitative methods. The remainder of this chapter identifies the wide variety of methods and data commonly used to address the big questions in higher education settings and considers the strengths and limitations of each.

Access

Access to higher education is discussed in terms of who applies to, is admitted to, and enrolls in college, often particularly in regard to underrepresented groups; this information is critical to colleges and universities, nationally and to individual institutions. Quantitative methodologies such as counts or metrics and surveys are the most commonly used research designs to address these questions.

The counts or metrics of the number of students who applied, were admitted, and enrolled (i.e., the yield) are relatively easy to tabulate; data such as these may be included on an institution's dashboard. Dashboards are graphical presentations of key indicators that are easy to understand at a glance; the indicators are derived from existing data and statistics contained in census, archival, or secondary datasets. The dashboards commonly found in colleges and universities take their data from student information systems. Institutions frequently have an array of dashboards to address a variety of foci, such as dashboards that present information about applicants and admitted students (to serve admissions offices and disciplinary departments), enrolled students (to serve the registrar's office, advising offices, and departments), and employees (to serve human resources). Much of the information presented includes counts or metrics that may have involved some statistical analysis, from the simple (percentages) to more complex (regression). For example, a strategic enrollment management process tabulates enrollment metrics across a variety of student characteristics, especially in terms of gender, race, ethnicity, age, native/international, and perhaps other important traits such as test scores, grade point average (GPA), or high school. Strategic enrollment management also frequently includes some advanced analyses using inferential statistics, modeling, and regression to identify methods for improving the yield generally and perhaps specifically in terms of diversity in the student body.

For researchers, these counts and metrics, whether presented on dashboards or not, are existing data, also referred to as secondary data, that have been collected at an earlier point in time by someone other than the current researcher (Johnson & Christensen, 2004). They can be used for testing hypotheses, exploring theories, generating future research ideas, and supporting original data collected (Black & Champion, 1976); secondary data are particularly valuable because they save time, as the data are already collected. However, the user or researcher has no control over, or even knowledge about, how the original data were collected. In addition, their presentation may not be useful to the questions of interest as the data may not fit the topic or question, thereby forcing the researcher to adjust the project scope to fit the data (Black & Champion, 1976); without access to the original data, the researcher may be stymied. Finally, although valuable in providing answers to specific, often narrow, questions, once the analyses are complete and an institution knows who is enrolling, none of those quantitative analyses can uncover *why* those students are enrolling; that is, why do they want to pursue a college degree, and why at that institution? Nor do they tell us why students drop out, stop out, or flunk out.

Surveys provide answers to those questions and others that seek to understand a participant's thoughts, feelings, behaviors, attitudes, values, personality, or perceptions (Johnson & Christensen, 2004). Surveys and questionnaires are instruments that collect self-reported data from participants by using mostly closed-ended questions that can be automatically coded (Given, 2008). Researchers can survey a national sample or the population from a single institution. For instance, the Higher Education Research Institute (HERI) at UCLA, through its Cooperative Institutional Research Program (CIRP), has surveyed first-year students (formerly known as freshmen) students for 50 years. The 2015 sample was selected from a population of 1.5 million first-year students at 1,574 4-year institutions across the United States (Eagan et al., 2016).

With respect to questions of access to college in terms of "Who gets a college education?" these students who enrolled thought it was very important to go to college in order to be able to get a better job (86% of first-year students at public universities), to learn more about things that interest them (84%), to gain training for a specific career (75%), to gain a general education and appreciation of ideas (71%), to be able to make more money (70%), to prepare themselves for graduate or professional school (60%), or to make them a more cultured person (49%) (Eagan et al., 2016, p. 48). Clearly, this national sample found that first-year students are career oriented and less concerned about becoming liberally educated students; they go to college to get a better job, get career training, and make more money. Institutions of higher education are also curious about why students choose their particular schools. The results from that same CIRP national survey of a sample of first-year students indicates that the following are very important reasons for choosing a college (Eagan et al., 2016, p. 51): academic reputation (73%), good jobs obtained by graduates (60%), good reputation for social activities (48%), financial assistance offered (47%), and cost of attendance at the college (44%). Again, career and academic concerns drove students' choice of institutions, followed by economic realities. Similar results were found at Old Dominion University (ODU). Each year we use our own Transition to College Inventory (TCI) to survey the entire first-year cohort—that is, the population. Like the national sample, ODU first-year students go to college generally, and choose ODU specifically, primarily for career, academic, and economic reasons.

Surveys such as the CIRP and TCI have significant strengths and important weaknesses. Many characteristics can be measured by one survey, and closed questions are typically very easy to administer and complete (Black & Champion, 1976). When the samples are carefully drawn to be representative of a larger population, researchers may be able to generalize findings and deduce cause-and-effect relationships (Creswell, 2014). These strengths, particularly the ease of survey administration and data coding, make surveys a very popular tool, and they are the most common method of data collection

(Given, 2008). Their wide use, however, has led to declining response rates as students get bombarded with survey requests. Misleading responses increase with the number of required surveys as students resist, and with longer questionnaires as respondent fatigue sets in (Black & Champion, 1976). Finally, closed-ended surveys limit the choices available to those selected by the researcher; when choices do not adequately reflect participants' experiences, they may simply "check a box" to be done.

Beyond the metrics and survey results, other research methods might contribute to the discussion about access. For example, one of the key concerns about access applies to underrepresented groups such as poorer students; racial and ethnic minority students; and, in some disciplines, women. This focus leads to the research questions: How do we identify more underrepresented groups of students and inspire them to apply; once admitted, how do we encourage them to enroll; once enrolled, how do we help them succeed? Neither the metrics nor the survey results help much to answer those questions. An institution could attempt a quasiexperimental design wherein it would identify matched groups of students who did and did not go to college from a particular high school and then examine differences between the two groups and make plausible causal inferences and test theory (Johnson & Christensen, 2004). However, participants may not be a representative sample of the population, and they are not randomly assigned to groups (Parker, 1993). In addition, confounding or extraneous variables cannot be controlled. As a result, any interpretation is ambiguous since the effect that occurred (college attendance) may be explained by alternative possibilities (Johnson & Christensen, 2004; Parker, 1993; Shadish, Cook, & Campbell, 2002).

Clearly, counts or metrics and surveys provide important information about access, but they simply cannot answer every question. Indeed, it is possible that they offer the least about the most important questions surrounding access to higher education. It is here that qualitative methods such as interviews and focus groups provide needed insight.

Interviews are a more valuable method of learning more about who does not apply and why. *Interviews* are "a basic mode of inquiry" (Seidman, 2013, p. 8) and defined as a professional conversation between a participant and a researcher about a specified topic (Kvale & Brinkmann, 2009); another definition is a coordinated conversation "between two unacquainted individuals" (Gubrium & Holstein, 2001, p. 57). Interviews allow a researcher to gather data about how participants make meaning about a topic of interest because interviews explore people's experiences, thoughts, or behaviors in depth and allow individuals to tell their stories (Seidman, 2013). The information collected in interviews is more detailed than survey data (Boyce & Neale, 2006), and so it can help us discover the experiences, fears, and realities that serve as barriers to college access. For participants whose responses are expected to be particularly valuable but who are uncomfortable with a group setting, interviews can be used as an alternative to focus groups. Interviews can also be used in an exploratory nature to gather information needed to construct a survey, or they can provide context as a follow-up to help explain the results of a survey (Boyce & Neale, 2006).

Interviews are often the foundation of a case study. Case studies are qualitative descriptive research projects that provide detailed analyses of an individual unit (e.g., a person or program) within its particular context. They generally involve a variety of data collection methods including interviews, observations, and content analysis of documents. A case study investigating the big question of access might dig deep into the success of a particular institution. For example, Xavier University of Louisiana is a historically Black college and university with 3,000 students, most of whom are first-generation college students from low-income backgrounds with the poor educational experiences that often accompany the intersection of class and race. And yet, Xavier has for decades sent more African American students to medical school than any other college or university in the country (Hannah-Jonessept, 2015). Analysis from interviews identified a range of reasons for Xavier's success, most of which are related to an intense focus on collaboration among faculty and students geared to student success. Xavier faculty work together to plan and teach a highly structured curriculum with frequent assessments, students form peer mentoring study groups and help one another succeed, and a pre-med advising office works closely with students to begin preparing application materials and for the MCAT almost from the start of their college education. The intense attention and the relationships that develop as a result both ensure student success at Xavier and increase the likelihood of success in medical schools with little or no support structure for African American students. Understanding Xavier's success in order to replicate it is simply not possible using only quantitative data; interviews are required to provide the context and complete the picture.

However, because they are one-on-one conversations, interviews are extraordinarily labor intensive and expensive in terms of time and perhaps money (Seidman, 2013). If conducted by multiple interviewers who will not analyze the data, the interviews must be recorded and transcribed prior to analysis. Information gathered from a small group of selected interviewees only comes through the lens of each individual and therefore is not generalizable (Boyce & Neale, 2006; Creswell, 2014).

A better solution would be to randomly select small groups of high school seniors or first-year students who are members of underrepresented groups to engage in small focus group discussions to help uncover the deeper meanings behind college nonattendance:

- What is keeping you from applying to college?
- How important is it to you to attend college?
- How important is it to your family?
- What appeals to you about attending college?
- What worries you about attending college?
- What are the chances you will be successful in college?
- What would you be doing now if you chose not to attend college?

It is only through qualitative methods such as individual interviews or small, focus group discussions that we can learn of the fears, hopes, and dreams that young people carry that might inhibit them from attempting college or engaging with their education once they arrive on campus, and the strategies that might help them succeed. The qualitative data collected help us appreciate how these young people make sense of the everyday world they inhabit and the world they contemplate. With respect to access, counts and metrics are useful for describing a population, but it is qualitative data that help us *understand* that population and the challenges they encounter, and how to build the pathways to success.

Affordability

Another group of big questions considered by governments and students for higher education today surrounds affordability: How much does college cost? How much of the cost will be the responsibility of students and their families versus governments? How are students paying for college? How much debt will students accrue across four (or five, or six) years of college? What is the default rate among students who have loans? And, how many students leave without graduating because of anticipated debt? Certainly, federal and state governments regularly express alarm about the cost of college, but individual institutions are also concerned about controlling costs while still providing a good education. And students are certainly anxious about both current costs and future debt. All of these measures are collected from colleges, governments, and individual students and then compiled into databases. Once again, many of the questions can be answered quantitatively using existing data. Federal and state governments as well as institutions can then create dashboards to monitor and report the metrics.

Each year the National Center for Education Statistics (NCES) publishes a report on *The Condition of Education*. The most recent report, published in 2017, offers a wealth of data on affordability, including the price of attending, number of grants, percentage of student loans and the default rate, plus college and university revenues and expenses. Including the costs of tuition and fees, books and supplies, room and board, and other expenses, the cost for attending a four-year institution among first-time, full-time undergraduates in 2014–2015 was $13,200 for public institutions (in state), $25,400 for private institutions, and $21,500 for for-profit institutions (NCES, 2017, p. 276).

The high cost of college means that while some students and their parents pay the full amount, the vast majority require some form of financial aid, which can prove burdensome. Indeed, NCES reported that 86% of undergraduate students in 2014–2015 received financial aid, either as grants that do not require repayment or as loans that must be repaid (NCES, 2017, p. 144). Loans represent a significant concern for students. Nearly one-half (47%) of all students received loans, which averaged $7,000 (an increase of $1,900 since 2000–2001); 14% of students who received loans defaulted on them (NCES, 2017, pp. 282–283).

The reliance on loans began in the 1980s. Prior to then colleges were largely supported by government funding; tuition was affordable, and individual financial aid was almost wholly in the form of grants. Attacks on government and the public sector fueled the shift from state and federal funding of higher education to student funding. While higher education benefits the entire society, some legislators suggested that the benefit accrues primarily to students, so they should fund their own educations (Mitchell & Leachman, 2015). Thus, legislators have made individual students responsible for college costs and done so increasingly in the midst of the economic crisis and following the decades-long working- and middle-class wage stagnation. The heavy reliance on loans exacerbates the stress students experience, and in some cases leads to dropping out, most likely occurring among first-generation and poorer students, as well as students from underrepresented racial and ethnic minority groups.

In April 2014 *The Chronicle of Higher Education* announced the publication of 15 papers sponsored by the Lumina Foundation discussing college affordability; student-loan repayment options; and institutional, state, and federal partnerships (Keierleber, 2014). Most of the papers used quantitative analyses and many used big data to support a variety of perspectives about making higher education more affordable. About half of the articles in this series discussed affordability specifically. Collectively they worked on defining *affordability*, including the different impacts on different students, especially low-income students; cost-benefit analyses of financial aid; the impact of politics on the distribution of aid from the federal government down through the institutional level; and recommendations for improvements. Affordability cannot be discussed without also focusing on student loans and related debt. Thus, the focus of one-third of the articles was on analysis of various loan repayment options along with the costs and benefits of each. And once again one might ask, how would these studies and recommendations be informed by analyzing the conversations of students involved in focus group discussions?

In short, quantitative analyses of large national databases suggest that the price of a college education is escalating, an increasing number of students require financial aid to pay their college expenses, and the percentage of students dependent on loans is increasing. At the same time, public support for higher education is stagnant or declining, forcing more of the cost onto students. All of this is helpful information; however, making it more meaningful and actionable, especially on the institutional level, requires information from students about the impact of costs on their ability to continue attending college, graduate, and repay their debt while beginning a career.

What other research questions might inform this discussion about affordability? With college costs rising and an increased dependence on financial aid, it seems logical to ask: How many students are working to pay college costs? How many hours per week? On or off campus? To what extent is work interfering with students' academic progress? Are they working primarily to pay tuition and fees or extracurricular activities? Surveys often explore the impact of work on students. Moore and Rago (2007) used National Survey of Student Engagement (NSSE) data to explore what prompts students to work either on or off campus, students' motivations for working, and the subsequent impact of working on student engagement. Three-quarters of students worked either on (32%) or off campus (41%) in order to pay for school expenses, living expenses, and entertainment expenses; to support their families; and to gain work experience in their career fields. Working on campus tended to enhance engagement in the five benchmarks of effective educational practice measured by the NSSE (Level of Academic Challenge, Active and Collaborative Learning, Student and Faculty Interaction, Enriching Educational Experiences, and Supportive Campus Environment), while working off campus—which the majority of students did—tended to decrease engagement in those five benchmarks.

While the analysis of the NSSE survey data offers helpful information to the conversation about students' motivations to work and the potential impact of working on their engagement in college, other questions still need to be explored to understand more extensively how affordability issues influence students' college decisions and academic success. Once again we can learn from interviews or focus group discussions with randomly selected high school or college students in which we ask them questions like the following:

- What is the value of a college education to you? To your family?
- What are the knowledge, skills, and abilities you are learning, or expect to learn, that will help you in your career?
- How big a factor were college costs in deciding to attend or remain in college?

- To what extent do financial concerns have an impact on your ability to be successful academically?
- To what extent is the cost and all of the work required worth the value of a college degree?

Clearly affordability is a complex issue that would benefit from multiple perspectives. The wealth of quantitative data available explains some of the problems with financing and paying for a college education. However, quantitative data alone do not answer questions about the impact of cost, working, and loans on student success. Qualitative data gathered in focus groups allows for deeper understanding of student experiences and potential solutions.

Accountability

Accountability in higher education is often associated or perhaps confused with other concepts such as assessment, accreditation, outcomes, outputs, and student success. Academic performance, retention, persistence, and graduation rates are considered to be critical measures of an institution's success. Other factors include how many graduates get jobs in their fields of study and what their starting salaries are. As is the case with access and affordability, many of these data can be collected and tallied quantitatively even if some, like salary data, are difficult to collect. They can also be added to a dashboard or scorecard for quick review by high-level administrators and legislators.

Retention of new students from one fall semester to the next fall semester and graduation rates from the same school within six years are among the most important measures of higher education productivity. According to the NCES (2012), the retention rate for fall 2011 (i.e., retention to fall 2012) full-time, first-time, degree-seeking students enrolled in a four-year degree-granting institution was 80%. More than half (59%) of first-time, full-time, degree-seeking students who entered a four-year institution completed a degree at the same institution within six years (NCES, 2015). Graduation rates differ for women (62%) and men (56%) (NCES, 2015), and for African American (39%) and White students (62%) (NCES, 2012).

With respect to job placement and salary, national data indicate that individuals with a bachelor's degree have higher employment rates (NCES, 2015). They also "earned more than twice as much as those without a high school credential ($48,500 versus $23,900) and 62 percent more than young adult high school completers ($48,500 versus $30,000)" (NCES, 2015, p. xxix). Federal and state officials pressure institutions to report job placement rates and graduates' salary information for comparison; national data are valuable yet each institution creates its own survey, asks questions of graduates differently, and may have low response rates. Job placement rates can be misleading or difficult to interpret, so they rarely offer useful information, especially in terms of comparability. In sum, metrics such as retention, graduation, job placement, and salary rates do not give meaningful information about how well students are prepared for the workplace or how well they perform in the workplace.

Assessing student learning can be a way of gathering more information about how well higher education institutions are preparing students for the workplace and beyond. Student learning as an accountability measure has the potential to inform the public about how well institutions are performing in terms of what they are teaching students and whether the students are gaining essential skills, but developing valid and reliable measures of student learning is challenging. *Academically Adrift: Limited Learning on College Campuses* by Arum and Roksa (2010) attempted to address the quality of higher education by investigating students' academic expectations and academic gains. The authors asked: "How much are students actually learning in contemporary higher education?" (Jaschik, 2011). They concluded that student "gains in critical thinking, complex reasoning, and written communication are either exceedingly small or empirically nonexistent" (Arum & Roksa, 2011, p. 36), since at least 45% of students did not demonstrate statistically significant improvement in learning skills over two years, and 36% did not demonstrate improvement over four years.

Academically Adrift rocked higher education and provided fodder to politicians and pundits seeking reasons to cut funding due to accountability failures. But what does the study really say about the quality of higher education? What does a standardized pre- and posttest design tell anyone (faculty, administrators, parents, or policymakers) about the quality of higher education? Is this a true snapshot of higher education's contribution to society?

As with most quasiexperimental studies, this research encountered many limitations. Certainly, the study's conclusions were challenged in discussions about the realities of mass testing without consequences. Students did not take the test seriously as it was unrelated to any concern of theirs, their score had no personal repercussions, and they may not have ever learned their scores. The students were not randomly selected to participate, so the sample may not have been representative. In addition, there was limited control of confounding or extraneous variables, such as motivation or learning environment. Therefore, conclusions that determined a cause-and-effect relationship without considering other plausible alternative explanations were inappropriate and created ambiguous interpretations (Johnson & Christensen, 2004; Parker, 1993; Shadish et al., 2002).

The questionable results attributed to *Academically Adrift* led researchers to turn to employer surveys to learn more about what institutions are doing to prepare students. According to a 2013 survey of employers conducted by the Association of American Colleges & Universities (AAC&U), the majority of companies want a workforce with skills that drive innovation. Specifically, employers agree that "a candidate's demonstrated capacity to think critically, communicate clearly, and solve complex problems is more important than his or her undergraduate field of study" (Hart Research Associates, 2013, p. 4). When asked how well higher education institutions are doing in preparing students for economic success, the majority of employers responded "good job" (47%) or "excellent" (9%). Furthermore, two-thirds of employers feel that students have the skills and knowledge to obtain and succeed at an entry-level job, although fewer employers (44%) believe students have the ability to advance or be promoted within the company (Hart Research Associates, 2013).

Without question, surveys are useful, but there are limitations to the data. Respondents are limited to the item choices selected by the researcher, and respondent fatigue may occur with longer questionnaires, resulting in responses that may be misleading (Black & Champion, 1976). The limitations of surveys and metrics point to the need to collect qualitative data on student learning and performance in the workplace.

In order to address the accountability question in terms of student learning, focus groups with employers can be conducted to identify knowledge, skills, abilities, and attitudes of successful graduates and assess how well the program prepared graduates to be successful practitioners. Focus groups give a deeper understanding of what students need to learn and be able to do to be successful in the workplace. Knowledge gained can inform changes and improvements to the curriculum that would enhance student success in the workplace. Employers can be asked questions, such as the following:

- What knowledge, skills, abilities, and attitudes/values characterize successful employees?
- To what extent do graduates possess or demonstrate the knowledge, skills, abilities, and attitudes/values of successful employees?
- What are specific areas of strengths or weaknesses that seem to recur?
- What can the program do to improve the curriculum or teaching methods?
- If you had one recommendation for the program, what would it be?

The promise of higher education is to educate students, that is, to enhance student learning. The focus on metrics, such as job placement and retention and graduation rates, provides limited insight into the accountability question, Does college deliver on its promise? Retention, graduation, job placement, and salary data are not proxies for learning; they do not demonstrate that students have learned the skills employers are seeking. Surveys of employers provide some information about student learning, but as indirect measures they are not authentic assessments of learning. Simply put, these data are incomplete. The voices of faculty, students, and employers are missing. These voices help answer accountability questions and tell stakeholders what students have learned and what led them to success. A more accurate picture of higher education's promise is found in hearing from students how well they learned and can apply transferable skills, such as communication and critical thinking, and asking them to demonstrate those skills; or hearing faculty discuss their educational practices. Hearing from students about what helped them be successful gives deeper meaning to an 80% retention rate or 59% graduation rate. Qualitative data give meaning and context to job placement and salary data and can help institutions develop programs and services to help students or identify populations that may need additional assistance.

About Validity, Reliability, and Generalizability

Analysis of focus group data often requires balancing rigor and relevance, so it mirrors the debate between quantitative and qualitative research. Quantitative research is considered by many to be the sine qua non of reliable and valid research because of its rigorous practices and procedures designed to reduce bias. In addition, quantitative research produces numbers that are subject to statistical analyses using computers. The production of tables, equations, and statistical significance often implies greater reliability and validity. In reality, however, quantitative research that focuses almost exclusively on rigor may actually be less relevant in that it is no longer concerned foremost with observations of people operating in real-world circumstances. Qualitative research, in contrast, is considered by many to be not only less rigorous but also more relevant as it seeks to observe people operating in real-world experiences. Thus, it is incumbent on quantitative research to defend its relevance while qualitative research must defend its rigor.

Creswell (2014) helped to define and defend the rigor of qualitative research. He framed the quantitative concepts of reliability and validity in qualitative terms and discussed how they can be applied to qualitative research so as to appease our more quantitatively oriented colleagues. Several of his points can be applied specifically to focus group research. As explained by Creswell (2014), "qualitative validity means that the researcher checks for the accuracy of the findings by employing certain procedures" (p. 201).

Researchers are attempting to show that the data and results are trustworthy, authentic, and credible. This is accomplished through a variety of techniques including (a) triangulating with related quantitative data; (b) "member checking," which can be accomplished through town hall meetings in focus group research; (c) using thick, rich description of the focus group themes; (d) including negative or discrepant data that may contradict the themes; and (e) debriefing the moderators of each segment. Each of these techniques individually, and certainly through various combinations, helps to enhance trustworthiness, authenticity, and credibility of the analyses.

With respect to reliability in qualitative research, Creswell (2014) stated that "qualitative reliability indicates that the researcher's approach is consistent across different researchers and different projects" (p. 201). Thus, when conducting focus groups we use a common Moderator's Guide that is edited and has been through numerous drafts to ensure that the questions are asked in ways that elicit responses that will address the research questions and the topic. We also carefully select moderators and train them to use the Moderator's Guide so that all participants are asked the same questions in the same manner. Finally, the moderators use the Moderator's Guide as the template to conduct their analyses so the data are interpreted according to the same format.

Generalizability in quantitative research refers to the study's results being applicable to a usually much larger population because the methodology ensures a sample that is representative of the population. In contrast, Creswell (2014) defined *generalization* in qualitative research as reflecting a specific and particular group, organization, or experience; he embraced the term *particularity* to refer to the qualitative research results that apply to a specific or particular context. Using thick, rich description of the themes related to each of the topic questions, focus group moderators and the Focus Group (FG) Expert attend to the details of a particular situation or topic with a specified group of participants, particularly within population segments. If the themes from all of the segments are similar, then we consider them to be accurate; we could speak of them as generalizable, though we do not use that language. If people from other institutions read the Research Proposals and Moderator's Guides, they can determine the extent to which they have similar populations and settings and consider whether the themes reported in the findings might apply to their settings. In this way, generalization is in the eye of the beholder.

The ODU Method is designed to apply Creswell's (2014) principles to produce results that are rigorous as well as relevant. The moderators are the research tool or instrument who use a common Moderator's Guide to ask the questions and listen carefully to, and take a few notes during, the discussion among participants. After the groups are completed, moderators reflect on the discussions, review their notes, and listen to the recordings to search for themes that emerge from the data. The process is carefully designed to produce consistent results through the use of trained moderators all using the same Moderator's Guide. The data analysis process produces accurate, rigorous, and credible results because moderators use the Moderator's Guide as a template and check data against notes and recordings as well as between and among co-moderators. All of these techniques are designed to reduce the bias that is inherent when doing research at one's own institution, or what Creswell (2014) called "backyard" (p. 188) research. The FG Expert takes care not to bias the research or compromise anyone's confidentiality when choosing moderators, selecting the setting for focus groups, discussing the importance of confidentiality in the Moderator's Guide, and analyzing the data.

As a final check, clients are encouraged to hold town hall meetings with representatives of each segment during which the results are shared and participants are invited to comment and ask questions. We could also consider using an electronic town hall meeting in which the results are e-mailed to the segment (e.g., faculty) or posted on their constituency's website (e.g., faculty senate website) for a limited time and members are invited to make comments, ask questions, or make suggestions for improvements. Thus, following the ODU Method for conducting focus groups leads to consistent and accurate data and results.

2

USING FOCUS GROUPS TO LISTEN, LEARN, AND LEAD

The ODU Method for Conducting Focus Groups

A discussion about retention and graduation rates began during a president's cabinet meeting. Confusion reigned as to why the rates were flat or declining at the university. Admissions tests were repeatedly analyzed and 10-year student demographic trends were scrutinized, but no one could figure out why students were leaving the university. After the cabinet meeting, a vice president walked down to the assessment office and said, "We're admitting these bright kids who are exactly the ones we want, and they're failing their courses. What's going on here? You need to figure this out, and fast!"

"Necessity is the parent of invention" and the ODU Method of conducting focus groups was developed out of both necessity and curiosity. In the late 1980s and early 1990s, members of the ODU Team sought to gain a better understanding of student success. All members of the ODU Team of assessment staff and institutional researchers were steeped in quantitative research methods and some were also trained as counselors with experience in student services. The questions of concern included: Why did some students who were predicted to be successful complete the semester in academic difficulty? And why were other students who were predicted to be at risk actually quite successful? These were the questions that led to the development of our TCI. Higher education researchers have sought answers to these questions for years through a variety of statistical analyses. In developing the TCI, we followed what seemed to be the standard practice, using multiple and logistic regression procedures to test the impact of academic factors using metrics such as high school GPA and standardized admission test scores, plus demographic factors like gender and race, on academic performance and retention. Though replete with quantitative data and impressive in their statistical prowess, these regressions typically explained less than one-third of the variance. The counselors among us felt that there might be some "noncognitive" or "affective" factors (e.g., motivation or commitment to the student role) related to academic performance and retention that might add to the predictive ability, and thus the TCI survey was born. We factor analyzed the TCI and found a satisfactory nine-factor solution. We also looked at the relationship of the answers to each item with academic performance and developed a TCI score that we used to identify high-, medium-, and low-risk first-year students. As counselors, we wanted to do more than merely identify at-risk students, so we worked with colleagues in the counseling center and academic advising to develop protocols for working with these students, and we tested those protocols. As rich as all of these data were, we knew our work could be improved with some in-depth discussions with those first-year students who were identified as high risk versus those who were identified as low or medium risk.

At the same time we were learning more about qualitative research methods, both as participants in workshops and classes and as faculty teaching courses. It became clear that qualitative research might be more *relevant* to in-depth questions about student success, but we wondered if it was a sufficiently *rigorous* approach to research in terms of attention to methodological details. The ODU Team, trained in quantitative research methods, was well acquainted with the rigorous part of research with human subjects. Yet, as counselors we constantly questioned the limitations of the data collected and the artificial situations in which quantitative research was typically conducted. We wondered if we could conduct research in ways that might elicit greater depth of information and in more realistic circumstances, such as meeting students where they lived and relaxed, socialized, studied, and attended class. And, could this type of research be conducted with sufficient rigor that it would be accepted by our colleagues and supervisors? Hadley and Mitchell (1995) summarized the dilemma nicely, stating,

> solving one design problem usually creates others. Tightly controlled experiments maximize internal validity, though they sacrifice external validity because laboratories differ from the kinds of settings in which counseling takes place. Field studies may maximize external validity, but the kinds of controls necessary for strong internal validity are difficult if not infeasible. (p. 225)

Given our intent, qualitative research methods emerged as an appealing answer to our questions about student success. Specifically, focus groups offered us the opportunity to engage students in structured conversations among themselves while we listened. We conducted six focus groups with six to eight students and asked them a variety of questions designed to elicit their thoughts about their academic experiences. We wanted to learn not only about student success but also how to help students identified as at risk; we decided that the best way to do this would come from those very students. Therefore, toward the end of these first focus groups we asked students, "What would you do differently if you had it to do over again?" or "What would you recommend to the next class of first-year students?" We further developed the ODU Method in a series of relatively small projects. From first-year and transfer students we sought to learn about their transition to and first year experiences at the university. We also talked to faculty and staff to assess the quality of their work life. These projects developed our expertise and made us the go-to people for focus groups on campus.

> Less than two months after the new president arrived on campus, Worth was walking up the steps in the administration building when the provost stopped him, handed him a piece of paper, and said, "The president wants the answers to these questions for her inauguration in two months. She wanted to bring in some outsiders to do focus groups, but I told her that we've got the expertise right here . . . and that's you!"

The ODU Team started developing Research Proposals when we were asked by a new president to conduct focus groups, first among her university leadership team at a summer retreat and subsequently among faculty, staff, and students during the fall semester. The focus groups were to provide data on "our" (faculty, staff, and students) vision for the university for the president to use in her inaugural address to the campus in early October.

The project began during the president's administrative retreat attended by the senior leadership of the university, where we assembled seven groups for a five-hour-long discussion during one day, analyzed the data that evening, and then presented the results to the same group the next morning. Because we could not invite anyone outside of the president's list, we lacked a sufficient number of experienced moderators, and so we trained several participants in advance as moderators. We also used co-moderators to balance expertise, workload, gender, and ethnicity. Because the president wanted a quick turnaround on the analyses, we designed a method of using the co-moderators to complete the first phase of the analyses, in effect serving as the research tool. And we presented the analyses back to the group the next day for validation. When one participant said, "I think you nailed it" and others nodded their agreement, we knew we had a good method, one that was relevant and rigorous.

Our work at the retreat was so successful that when we returned to campus we were given less than a month to conduct focus groups among faculty, administrative and classified staff, and undergraduate and graduate students and report the results to the president so that she could incorporate them into the vision statement for her inauguration. Our investment of work over the years with smaller projects, followed by the leadership retreat with its immediate data analysis requirement, prepared us for this massive undertaking. This was the largest project we had ever done, and it occurred in a very short time frame; it ultimately involved 29 focus groups, with 290 participants and 50 moderators, over 6 weeks. Achieving this required excellent communication and coordination among a large Research Team and many co-moderators. Perhaps more importantly, we needed to ensure that the Research Team was doing exactly what the president and her cabinet had asked us to do. The success of the overall project was largely due to the Research Proposal we developed that the president approved. While this was a large, high-stakes project, it makes sense to anyone trained in research methodology to develop a Research Proposal or plan to guide the work, and we nearly always do so for any focus group project we conduct.

In the following spring semester the president asked us to extend the focus groups to a variety of off-campus constituencies including surrounding communities, parents, high school faculty and staff, local business owners, and so forth. Approximately 2 years later she asked us to replicate the process once again to conduct a SWOT (strengths, weaknesses, opportunities, and threats) analysis to begin the process of revising the strategic plan. In short, several small projects of 6 to 8 groups each prepared us to conduct 3 major university-wide projects of 15 to 25 groups each and helped us to establish and refine the ODU Method of conducting focus groups.

Thus, the ODU Method emerged from the perfect storm of nearly equal parts dissatisfaction with the ability of existing quantitative data or data gathered in surveys to answer our research questions; the recognition that focus groups, when conducted systematically, are a rigorous and relevant research method; and the challenge of conducting many focus groups in a relatively short time frame. The ODU Method, invented out of necessity, has been proven time and time again as a consistent and accurate way to gather data to listen to our focus group participants and learn about them from their discussions so that we can lead initiatives to improve the environment.

Key Components of the ODU Method

While colleges and universities may not have the financial resources to hire consultants to conduct focus groups, they do have a unique set of resources that enable them to conduct focus group research. Colleges and universities are filled with people possessing advanced degrees who have been trained in research methods and who are skilled at leading group discussions. The daily work of both teaching and administrative faculty requires them to listen, take notes, ask questions, synthesize, and work with others; in short, to learn. In the case of focus groups, they are trying to learn about a particular issue in depth. As members of the higher education community, they are also knowledgeable about the context, language, nuances, and culture of the institution. Based on their knowledge of the community and culture of the institution along with their ability to listen to and learn from focus group participants, teaching and administrative faculty are uniquely qualified to lead change in their community and culture. Furthermore, professionals within organizations have a distinct investment in the outcome, as well as social and political capital that they both share and gain. This insider relationship brings complexities at times, but being able to connect the results with in-house knowledge makes the process that much more valuable.

The ODU Method combines the relevance of qualitative research with the rigor of quantitative research. Key components of the ODU Method include using co-moderators to lead the group, using co-moderators to conduct the initial thematic analyses, and using town hall meetings with the various constituencies to confirm the results and recommendations. To enhance the rigor of focus groups, we employ a common Moderator's Guide and use some quantitative techniques such as random sampling to identify participants. The ODU Method thus balances rigor and relevance.

We recommend using co-moderators to conduct focus groups. Working as a co-moderator gives new moderators some comfort when paired with a more experienced moderator. Co-moderators can take turns moderating and taking notes or listening. They can help each other out when the group starts to stray off topic or spend too much time on a particular topic. And they can help each other with challenging participants like one who wants to dominate the conversation or one who is leading the group astray. When it is time for data analyses, co-moderators offer two, sometimes slightly varied, points of view—occasionally hearing and seeing things a bit differently—leading to some good discussion about the themes heard in their group. One additional advantage of using co-moderators is the opportunity to address diversity issues within groups. We typically try to use female and male co-moderators as well as co-moderators of different ages and ethnicities or races. This practice gives the diverse populations with whom we work the opportunity to see some aspect of themselves in the moderators.

Most teaching and administrative faculty possess advanced degrees and some training in research methods in their disciplines. Because of this methodological background, moderators are trained to complete the initial thematic analyses. Upon completion, the Research Team conducts a focus group or debriefing with all of the co-moderators who worked with a particular project. The Research Team then completes the Final Report.

A final idea that ensures the relevance of qualitative research is to test the analyses with the constituencies from whom they are collected in town hall meetings. After conducting the focus groups for the president, we wanted to make sure that our findings and recommendations accurately represented the views expressed. Thus, we presented the results of the initial focus groups conducted as part of the administrative retreat back to the retreat participants the next day and asked for their verification. When we returned to campus and conducted the subsequent rounds of focus groups, we followed up with town hall meetings with the faculty senate, the Association of University Administrators, and the Hourly and Classified Employees Association as a final check. This feedback loop process has proven to be central in the implementation of focus groups on college campuses. Furthermore, we find that it builds a greater investment in the institution and appreciation for the diverse contributions of various stakeholders and wider involvement of the campus community.

What Makes the ODU Method Different?

We developed the ODU Method for conducting focus groups in a manner that fits the unique culture of higher education. Our work is informed by Greenbaum (1988), who offered a 10-step process for developing and conducting focus groups and analyzing the results that would seem to work well in a consultant–client model such as might occur in the business world or in other organizations that seek outside assistance for their focus groups (pp. 25–35). The ODU Method employs a research model with a leadership team to whom we refer here as "the ODU Team," "the Research Team," "the Team," or "FG Expert." The model we developed relies on the Team to develop the project, create the Moderator's Guide, recruit and train the moderators, and conduct the data analyses. This model thus requires fewer and somewhat different steps, resulting in a 6-step process that is the ODU Method:

1. Develop a Research Proposal, define the purpose of the project, and write research questions.
2. Select participants and subsets of participants.
3. Design the Moderator's Guide.
4. Select and train the moderators.
5. Conduct the focus groups.
6. Analyze the data and report the results.

While the six steps are numbered and discussed in this order in the following chapters, this is not a linear process. It is difficult to define the purpose of the project without having some discussion about the variety of individuals invited to participate. Research questions often turn into the topics included in the Moderator's Guide with some slight editing. In addition, as the topic questions in the Moderator's Guide are developed, we often return to revise the purpose of the project. Working on the Research Proposal also usually entails some discussion about who will be asked to moderate the groups. Thus, this process resembles most research that begins with an ideal model that is then refined to fit the reality of the situation and the resources available.

In addition to our extensive experience with focus groups, we have also completed a variety of projects that might more accurately be described as focused discussions rather than focus group projects. The essential difference is in the emphasis on the discussion versus the data collected. Focus groups are a qualitative research tool designed to collect and analyze data to answer specific research questions. In contrast, focused discussions emphasize the discussion and are less concerned with the actual data collected. Data may be collected and analyzed but only as a summary of the discussion rather than as an analysis of data to answer research questions. Three projects that might be characterized as focused discussions are

1. identifying, defining, and specifying actions related to Old Dominion's Quality Enhancement Plan (QEP) topic for our reaffirmation of accreditation with SACSCOC;
2. *A Conversation on What It Means to Be an Educated Virginian,* co-sponsored by the State Council for Higher Education in Virginia and the Virginia Assessment Group; and
3. our work with an international conference, *Improving Functional Outcomes for Amputees: A Collaborative Approach.*

In these focused discussions we used moderators trained in the ODU Method. They worked from a Moderator's Guide so that each group discussed the same topics, and they completed the initial thematic analysis. While we were not able to hold a town hall to confirm the results, we did report summaries of the conversations to the project leadership.

Our Use of Vignettes and Reference to Appendices

We developed three vignettes that appear in subsequent chapters to illustrate the decisions that must be made, from the initial inquiry about conducting a focus group to writing the Final Report. Drawn from our experience, they provide concrete examples of what clients often request, the confusions that frequently arise, and how realistic compromises must be sought and might be achieved. The vignettes address the three big questions in higher education today. "Shirley" is a vice president of student affairs chairing a student success committee concerned about declining retention rates; trying to understand why students leave the university after their first year reflects concerns about *accountability*, as some assume that students leave because the university is not delivering on its promises. "James," the director of undergraduate admissions, must address improving *access* to the university for members of underrepresented groups, particularly how to encourage their applications, increase their enrollment once admitted, and ensure success once they arrive on campus. Finally, "Chris," the associate vice president for enrollment management, in asking about the impact of working on or off campus on students' academic success, presents the example of *affordability*. Note that these clients are not necessarily aware that they are engaged in seeking answers to the big questions in higher education, but their concerns certainly reflect them.

Appendices are referenced in the following chapters. We provide 15 appendices that are templates or completed models of all aspects of the ODU Method. Included are templates and fully completed examples for each of the vignette projects.

3

STEP #1: DEVELOP A RESEARCH PROPOSAL, DEFINE THE PURPOSE, AND WRITE RESEARCH QUESTIONS

To Do or Not To Do a Focus Group

Rigorous and relevant focus groups begin with the Research Proposal. This chapter provides details about the first and most important step in conducting focus groups: developing a Research Proposal that defines the purpose and the research questions in order to determine the necessity and efficacy of a focus group. Every year the ODU Team receives requests to conduct focus groups—the "I want to do a focus group" call—to achieve purposes that, upon discussion, are uncertain or ill defined or for which focus groups are not the best method. Sometimes the call is made because focus groups seem like a "quick and easy" way to understand or solve a problem. Sometimes it may be because focus groups are all the rage. Thus, the chapter begins with the "I want to do a focus group call" vignette, wherein a vice president of student affairs has decided that a focus group will answer her questions and solve her problem. And let us be clear here: Focus groups are seen as providing answers to a problem within the institution. The questions that arise during the call demonstrate the creative thinking required to define the purpose and research questions that are necessary before making the decision whether or not to proceed with a focus group. This chapter describes a number of projects, their purposes, and corresponding research questions and explains why some projects moved forward to focus groups while others adopted other methods of data collection or were abandoned in their entirety.

Shirley, a vice president of student affairs, calls and after catching up for a few moments says, "I am calling to ask you about conducting some focus groups for a student success committee I am chairing for the president. We want to find out why so many students are leaving our institution so we can make recommendations for specific initiatives."

FG Expert: "Sounds like an important topic, Shirley. What has your committee learned thus far about student success? What do you hope to learn from conducting focus groups?"

Shirley: "Our retention rates are down and we want to do a focus group to find out why. Over the last few months, we have looked at a lot of data, including high school GPA, admission tests, semester GPA, satisfaction survey results, course grades, DFWI rates, major selection, plus gender and race and ethnicity, and we still do not have a good understanding of why students leave. The Institutional Research Office helped us understand the data they collect regularly and suggested that focus groups might be a good next step. They suggested that you are the FG Expert."

FG Expert: "Okay, what specifically do you want to know and from whom?"

Shirley: "We want to know why students are leaving after their first year."

FG Expert: "From whom—students who left? Currently enrolled students? Faculty and staff?"

Shirley: "Students who left; perhaps currently enrolled students; and now that you mention it, the faculty and staff perspectives are important as well."

FG Expert: "That's potentially a lot of focus groups, Shirley. Students who left are very difficult to contact. We have done exit surveys, but they get very low response rates, so it seems even more unlikely that these students would return to campus for a focus group. If you want to gather data from them, I would suggest doing another exit survey with some very good incentives."

Shirley: "Good point."

FG Expert: "Let's think for a few minutes about what you want to learn from currently enrolled students. What would you ask them?"

Shirley: "Hmm . . . why they stayed? What contributed to their success? Why do they think other students left? What do you think I should ask?"

FG Expert: "The literature says that academic and social integration are important factors in retention and student success, and our research indicates academic performance is related to attrition on our campus, so perhaps we should focus on academic and social concerns. Whose perspective is important to answer the questions? Students will have different perspectives from faculty or staff." (See Appendix B for the full proposal.)

The discussion with Shirley typically continues for 30 to 45 minutes and covers a variety of topics, probably all of the steps of the focus group process including the use of a Moderator's Guide, the selection of moderators for the groups, and the logistics for conducting the groups. After we cover most of the process, we close the conversation by asking Shirley to meet again with her team and develop a Research Proposal that will answer these questions. Shirley asks, "How do we do that?" The ODU Team designed a Research Proposal template (see Appendix A) to answer such questions; we also offer to attend Shirley's next meeting and help her staff work through the process and proposal.

The Research Proposal or plan includes everything needed to conduct the focus groups and no more. The template in Appendix A asks the following questions:

- Client: Who are the people who initiate the focus group project?
- FG Expert: Who are the consultants, the FG Experts?
- Purpose and Research Questions: Why are we conducting these focus groups? What do we want to learn?
- Participants: What are the population and segments from which the sample of participants is drawn? *Population* refers to all the members of a group, as in first-year students. *Segments* refers to subgroups within the populations, as in first-year students in academic difficulty and those in success. The number of segments determines the number of groups; generally, we run two to three groups for each segment. This then determines the number of participants.
- Moderators: Who are the best people to moderate the focus groups— faculty, staff, or students?
- Logistics: Where and when will the focus groups be conducted? What refreshments will be provided? What incentives, if any, will be offered?
- Data Analysis: What will the data analysis look like and how will it be reported? Who will do it?
- Time Line: Backing up from the date the report is due, what will be done when by whom?
- Costs: How much will all of this cost?

Because the answers to most of these questions will impact other questions, developing the Research Proposal is not a linear process. We often work back and forth among the various components of the Research Proposal. As with many research projects in higher education, we start off with the "ideal" plan and then gradually refine it to make it more realistic and doable with the time and money allotted. It should also be noted that we have outlined a very thorough Research Proposal. Although it is indeed important for the client and their team to answer all of these questions, every institution can modify the actual Research Proposal to meet its unique needs.

The Client, Other Stakeholders, and the FG Expert

The people who make the call, or who direct their representatives to make the call, are the *clients*. The clients initiate the project and are the content experts on what they want to learn more about or understand better through the use of one or more focus groups. Clients generally work with staff or committee members on the issues that led to the specific reasons for making the call. *Other stakeholders* are those who want the research conducted (e.g., the provost, dean, or director) or who are otherwise involved in the issue. While other stakeholders may become involved at any stage of the research process, they most often check in when reviewing the final draft of the Moderator's Guide or the Final Report.

The FG Expert is typically administrative faculty in the assessment or institutional research office or perhaps some faculty engaged in educational research. One or more FG Experts may work on any given project. The FG Expert is an expert in conducting research using a variety of methods, including focus groups. An FG Expert generally works with the clients to draft the Research Proposal.

The FG Expert and clients will include or add members who are willing and able to accomplish all of the tasks associated with conducting a successful focus group project.

Purpose Statement

Developing good purpose statements and research questions seems to be the most difficult part of the project for many clients, yet they are the most critical part of the Research Proposal because they guide the entire project. In general, purpose statements are intended to answer the following questions: Why are we conducting these focus groups? What do we want to learn? The answers to these questions imply the changes that will be made or actions taken based on the outcome of the focus groups. Research questions specifically define what it is we want to learn. The parts of the question then become the topics that are addressed in the questions that are actually discussed by the participants in the focus group.

The literature is replete with discussions and debates about the meaning of purposes versus goals, objectives, outcomes, and so on, far beyond the scope of this book. What is needed are common definitions of important terms. Our work is informed by Creswell's (2014) *Research Design: Qualitative, Quantitative, and Mixed Methods Approaches.*

Creswell (2014) prefers the term *purpose statement* to *goals* and argues that it "is the most important statement in the entire study, and it needs to be clear, specific, and informative" (p. 123). To this end, Creswell (2014) lists numerous points to be considered in writing the purpose statement for the focus group project. We include and expand on the most relevant of those points here. Purpose statements should

- focus on a single phenomenon, concept, or idea;
- identify the participants;
- use the word *purpose* to concentrate attention to this statement as the central controlling idea and reason for the group: "The purpose of this focus group is to_____";
- use action verbs to convey how learning about and understanding the problem will take place, such as *understand, develop, explore, examine the meaning of, discover,* and *obtain*; and
- provide a general working definition of the central phenomenon, concept, or idea in terms that will be easily understood by the focus group participants. (pp. 124–125)

Sample Purpose Statement

Once the FG Expert and Shirley have determined the focus of the project, it is time to specify the purposes. Note that whether it is written out or not, each of the following purpose statements begins with: "The purpose of this focus group is to _____":

1. learn from students why they decide to stay or leave the institution.
2. obtain student perceptions of the challenges of the undergraduate experience at the institution.
3. determine what resources students need to help them be successful.

Research Questions

Creswell (2014) also describes and offers guidelines for writing good qualitative research questions; we include and expand on the most relevant of the guidelines. Research questions should

- focus on a single phenomenon or concept;
- specify the participants;
- begin with the words *what* or *how* (*where, when,* or *who* may also be used);
- use exploratory verbs that tell the reader that the study will do the following: *report, describe, discover, seek to understand, explore;*
- use nondirectional exploratory verbs to describe the relationship you are trying to understand such as *affect, influence, impact, determine, cause,* and *relate;* and
- use open-ended questions. (pp. 139–141)

Sample Research Questions

The following research questions could apply to Shirley's project:

- What are some reasons that students chose to return to the university for a second year?
- What are some reasons students leave the university?
- How do students perceive the quality of the undergraduate experience at the university? What do students think/say about the academic experience?
- What did students find most challenging about their academic experience?
- What resources did students use for assistance with academics? What other resources do students need to help them be successful?
- What do faculty say about students who succeed/fail in their classes?

Participants

Chapter 4 explores in depth the details of how to select participants after identifying populations and segments. For our discussion at this point, the populations and segments need to be identified in the Research Proposal along with some idea of how they will be sampled. The key concern for the Research Proposal is determining how many focus groups will be conducted. The number of focus groups will affect how many individuals are invited, how many moderators are needed, whether or not each population requires a separate Moderator's Guide, and logistics for conducting the groups.

An ideal focus group size is 7 to 10 participants, and each segment of the population requires 2 to 3 focus groups. Determining how many individuals to invite is similar to the issue of response rates in quantitative survey research. Certainly not all those who are invited will attend, and some populations will have a higher (or lower) response rate than others. To complicate matters further, it is often unclear how responsive a particular population is likely to be even with the use of RSVP requests. As the subject matter expert, the client should have some idea of the population and its likely response rate, or the particular incentives that are likely to increase positive responses. Thus, we ask: How many participants need to be invited in order to get how many to RSVP, in order to get 7 to 10 to actually show up? In this regard, students are a particularly challenging population.

Moderators

Chapter 6 covers the selection and training of moderators in detail. The clients and FG Expert need to develop a plan for selecting and training them. Each group requires two moderators, or co-moderators. We use the term *moderators* when talking about all those who moderate, and *co-moderators* when speaking about the two moderators who work together on a particular focus group. One of the most common questions is, "Why do we use co-moderators?" We began using co-moderators when everyone was new to conducting focus groups and a bit uncomfortable with the process. Co-moderators offer each other comfort. We also learned that co-moderators sometimes offer different perspectives on what was said in the group. The different perspectives usually lead to good discussions between co-moderators and more accurate analyses. And, perhaps most importantly, co-moderators allow us to offer diversity in terms of gender and race and ethnicity for the group. This is a unique part of the ODU Method that has resulted in better focus groups for participants, more comprehensive data for analysis, and added accuracy for clients.

The client needs to decide if faculty, administrators, staff, graduate students, or undergraduate students will be asked to moderate the groups. Typically, we use faculty or administrators with terminal degrees to conduct focus groups with faculty. We also generally use graduate students to conduct focus groups with undergraduate students. The goal is to match moderators with the topic and the population. Thus, the question to the client is: Who are the moderators who will best connect with the participants discussing the topic?

One warning to clients is that they may never conduct their own focus groups because of the obvious bias involved and the potential dampening of participant responses. However, we usually train the clients and use them to moderate other focus group projects with which they are not involved. Clients who are trained as moderators have a greater understanding of and appreciation for the methodology and the work required. And they return the favor when another unit needs moderators for their focus groups.

Logistics

Logistics are covered in chapter 7. Many of the logistics are the same as what is required to host an important meeting. It is critical to identify small conference rooms with round or oval tables and comfortable seating for 7 to 10 participants and two moderators who will co-moderate the group. Clients are also encouraged to discuss the provision of snacks for the group and incentives. Typically, both are offered to focus group participants.

Data Analysis

Data analysis is covered in chapter 8. It is important to discuss with clients what the report will look like. Another unique part of the ODU Method is that co-moderators do much of the data analysis without transcribing the audio recording of the focus groups. Transcription takes significant time and money and is simply not required when there is a structured format (the Moderator's Guide) and trained co-moderators. Colleges and universities are full of smart faculty, staff, and students who are capable of leading good discussions and conducting thematic analyses with a little bit of training. The Moderator's Guide is generally used as a template, and each co-moderator is tasked to listen to the audio recording, review notes taken during the focus group, and type bulleted themes into the Moderator's Guide to answer each question. Co-moderators then meet with their partners to look for similarities and differences in their findings and produce a combined report. This step and subsequent steps provide an excellent opportunity for the co-moderators to discuss and debate their observations to produce more accurate analyses. The data analysis process continues within segments until as a last step the FG Expert conducts a "focus group" with all of the co-moderators to produce the Final Report.

Whenever possible the results are verified or checked for accuracy in some way by the participants or the populations they represent. One method of confirmation is "member checking," which can be done in several ways. The FG Expert can send a draft of the report back to the focus group participants and give them a short time to offer any feedback, clarifications, or critique. Another method we employ when possible is to hold a town hall meeting in which we present the data back to the participants and other members of the population they represent and invite them to comment and offer feedback. For example, after completing the analyses for the president's focus groups, we presented the results to their respective populations and representative bodies—the senior leadership, faculty senate, Association of University Administrators, and the Hourly and Classified Employees Association. Member checking is an excellent method for scrutinizing the results for accuracy. Indeed, at this point additional data may be collected from those who attend the town hall and included in the report, though marked as coming from the member-checking event.

Time Line

The Research Proposal specifies the deadline and to whom the report should be submitted. It takes time to plan, conduct, and analyze the data from focus groups, and the amount of time required varies. For example, once the president approved the proposal, the ODU Team conducted seven groups at the president's leadership retreat, analyzed the data, and presented the report to the president and her leadership team the next morning. A few months later in the fall semester we also conducted multiple focus groups with faculty, staff, and students and produced a report for the president for each cohort within a week. While doable, useful, and effective for the president, it was a grueling experience for the ODU Team. The deadlines were very challenging and not the kind of time line that is recommended. Taking two to four weeks to develop the Moderator's Guide, reserve the rooms, create the focus group schedule, and invite the participants is much more reasonable. Taking an additional two to four weeks to analyze and report the data is also much more realistic.

Obviously, the time line depends on how many groups are planned and how much time the clients have to devote to this project along with their other work. The other key factor is paying attention to the academic schedule—exams, spring or fall breaks, holidays, and so forth.

Costs

As noted in chapter 7, on logistics, the costs of conducting focus groups include

- incentives to participants (e.g., mugs, bookmarks, movie tickets),
- refreshments or meals for participants and moderators,
- supplies,

- printing and postage for invitations if mailed,
- moderators, and
- consultants.

Clients might question some of these expenses, especially for moderators; however, it is important to treat focus group participants and moderators well. Both are offering their time and expertise. Light snacks and drinks should be provided for all participants in the group, and sometimes a meal will be required. Focus group participants are typically rewarded for their participation, often with something small but meaningful and perhaps also with a lottery for a grand prize. Moderators will work about 9 to 12 hours for the first group from training through data analysis and an additional 5 hours for each subsequent group they moderate for a single project. They should be compensated at least minimally for their work, which is typically beyond their job descriptions. Paying moderators sends the message that you recognize the value of their time and effort; it also increases the likelihood that they will participate in the future.

Other Important Questions

Several other important questions to consider throughout the development of the Research Proposal are as follows:

- What decisions will be made based on the results? This is an important question to ask clients in the early stages of the project to help determine whether or not focus groups are the best methodology and whether or not the project is viable.
- Is this project of sufficient interest and breadth to generate 60 to 90 minutes of discussion among the participants? Will people want to talk about the topic enough to attend the group? The answer to this question about interest and breadth helps to determine if focus groups are the best methodology for answering the research questions. (Consider the following: Can we actually get 60 minutes of conversation from 18-year-olds about retention? Instead of talking about why they stayed, can we talk about the resources they need or want? What about the challenges and success they encountered during their first year?)
- Will the participants understand the project? Do they have sufficient knowledge to be able to discuss the concepts?

In the next chapter we discuss selecting participants, after which we should return to our Research Proposal, purpose statement, and research questions to make sure they are all in alignment with each other. The same is true after, or as a part of, each of the subsequent steps. We want to make sure that the central phenomenon, concept, or idea remains central.

James Vignette (Access)

James is the new director of undergraduate admissions tasked with improving access to the university to members of underrepresented groups such as poorer students; racial and ethnic minority students; and, in some disciplines, women. This purpose leads to the research question: How do we identify more underrepresented groups of students and inspire them to apply; once admitted, how do we encourage them to enroll; once enrolled, how do we help them succeed? The vignette illustrates how to help James take a very big topic with three parts—admission, enrollment, success—and focus on his key responsibility of enrollment and then identify who might be best suited to address that concern.

James: "I have been encouraged to call you to discuss how we can collect some data to learn how we identify more underrepresented groups of students and inspire them to apply; once admitted, how do we encourage them to enroll; and once enrolled, how do we help them succeed?"

FG Expert: "Wow, that is a big research project, James, perhaps three different albeit related research projects. They are all interesting and important topics, however. Please tell me a little more about what it is you want to learn and from whom."

James: "As you know, I was recently appointed as the new director of undergraduate admissions, and I have been trying to learn as much as I can about our incoming first-year classes. I was charged to increase the admission and enrollment of underrepresented groups on campus. I need some help learning about the culture at this institution and identifying potential issues regarding underrepresented groups. I understand that you have experience answering this type of question, primarily using focus groups, which sounds perfect to me."

FG Expert: "Answering these questions is probably my favorite part of my job. Focus groups are a great tool to use to collect data if they are able to answer your research question. So, let's discuss that a little more. For example, assuming for a moment that these are actually three different but related topics, where do you want to start? Which is most important— admission, enrollment, or success?"

James: "All of the above; I eventually need to focus on all of them. However, for now let's start with enrollment. Student success beyond enrolling the best candidates who are able to succeed is someone else's responsibility. And I am not sure I know enough about the communities from which we draw applicants (or fail to draw applicants) to know where to begin just yet. So, let's start with enrollment—once admitted, how do we get the best students to enroll?"

FG Expert: "Good choice. Now who do we want to talk to—applicants or enrolled students? Faculty and staff who work with underrepresented groups? High school counselors or faculty?"

James: "Again I am tempted to say all of the above, but I am assuming that you would say that is too many. However, all have important information to share from different perspectives. I think the most critical, and easiest to contact, are enrolled students from underrepresented groups. We seem to have a relatively small group of administrators and faculty who work with groups of underrepresented students, so perhaps we can add one group of them."

FG Expert: "Good observation, James; when we plan to do two groups per constituency, the number of focus groups grows quickly. And some of those constituencies, like potential applicants, are difficult to contact. So, the constituencies you have identified is a good place to begin. Now, what is the purpose? What do you want to ask them?"

As in the vignette with Shirley presented earlier in this chapter, the FG Expert immediately begins asking James questions to help him to focus his research. This is similar to what faculty do with students, especially graduate students who are developing proposals for theses or dissertations. And, as in the vignette with Shirley, the FG Expert will give James homework assignments to complete to gradually build the Research Proposal. In this case, James has gone from asking three broad research questions (How do we identify more underrepresented groups of students and inspire them to apply; once admitted, how do we encourage them to enroll; once enrolled, how do we help them succeed?) to a more focused question that can be reasonably achieved: How do we encourage admitted students from underrepresented groups to enroll at the university? If James had chosen to focus on the first topic (How do we encourage underrepresented groups to apply to the university?), the FG Expert would have helped James to gain access to the local school system, community college, or a community agency and train the institution's faculty, staff, or graduate assistants to conduct the focus groups in the schools. If he had chosen the third topic (How do we help underrepresented students to be successful at the university?), the FG Expert would have helped James to set up those groups.

Toward the end of their first conversation, the FG Expert asked James to work with his committee and determine what they would like to ask their enrolled students who are members of underrepresented groups. Their draft questions include the following:

- How important is it for students from underrepresented groups to attend college? This college?
- How important is it for their families?
- What worries students from underrepresented groups about attending college? This college?
- What can the faculty and staff do to help students from under-represented groups to be successful both academically and socially at this college?
- What are the chances students from underrepresented groups will be successful in this college?

These are research questions that become draft questions for the Moderator's Guide. The decision to focus on enrolled students along with the research questions will help the FG Expert assist James in progressing through the remaining steps of the focus group process. A copy of the full Research Proposal is in Appendix C.

Chris Vignette (Affordability)

Chris, the associate vice president for enrollment management, contacts the FG Expert about the possibility of conducting focus groups to learn about students' perceptions of the impact of working on or off campus on academic success. The FG Expert discovers that Chris and the committee have done quite a bit of work on predicting academic performance, retention, and graduation rates by using the quantitative data available through the institution's student information system along with results from the CIRP Freshman Survey and NSSE. Chris agrees to send their report to the FG Expert who, in turn, sends Chris some information about focus groups and agrees to attend the committee's next meeting to provide an overview of the focus group process, including summaries of all six steps. The committee then engages in a discussion about their plans for focus groups.

FG Expert: "Your report based on the data available is very thorough and makes a good case for conducting focus groups as a next step. As I understand it, the purpose of the focus groups is to learn (a) what is the cost of earning a college degree while spending many hours working; (b) other than earning money, what is the benefit of working while attending college; and (c) is there a difference depending on whether students work on or off campus and how many hours per week they work. You also have some good ideas for topic questions, although I have some edits to suggest for them."

Chris: "Thank you. In the process of analyzing and digesting all of the data, it became clear to us what additional information we would like to know. What are your concerns about our questions?"

- What is the value of a college education to you? To your family?
- How big a factor were college costs in deciding to attend or remain in college? This college?
- To what extent do financial concerns have an impact on your ability to be successful academically?
- What is the benefit of working while in college?
- To what extent is the cost and all of the work required worth the benefit of a college degree?
- What is the impact of working part-time on or off campus on your academic success?
- What are your career plans? What self- and career exploration have you done to confirm your choice? How committed are you to your career path?

FG Expert: "I am not sure how the last question about career plans fits in, although I agree it is an important question. I think the rest of the ideas are good and only require some fine-tuning. There also seems to be some redundancy in the questions and too many questions, so we need to work on combining and organizing them. Finally, I am sure that you understand what is being asked in these questions, but I am not sure they will be as clear to students."

Chris: "Are there other questions you would suggest?"

FG Expert: "I do not think you want more than four or five topic questions, so I would work on fine-tuning the questions you have proposed. The main question for you is if you have the answers to all of these questions, will you be able to answer your research questions?"

The conversation continues as the committee and FG Expert edit and debate the topic questions. The FG Expert tasks the committee to draft a Research Proposal for which the FG Expert provides a template (see Appendix A; Chris's Research Proposal is found in Appendix D). As they are drafting the Research Proposal, the FG Expert encourages the committee to include a few notes regarding each one of the steps, especially Step 2, selecting participants, which they agree to discuss at their next meeting.

4

STEP #2: SELECT
PARTICIPANTS AND SUBSETS
OF PARTICIPANTS

Choose Wisely

Rigorous and relevant focus groups depend on getting the appropriate people to participate. This chapter explains the importance of identifying the population that possesses the information desired at the depth needed (e.g., faculty, staff, or students) as well as identifying the segments of the population whose differing characteristics might result in varied opinions about the research purpose (e.g., tenured, tenure-track, or adjunct faculty; administrators; staff; undergraduate or graduate, first-year or transfer students). This chapter also covers how to select individuals within the segments to participate and proven methods to achieve the level of participation required.

After the research questions have been created, the conversation with Shirley moves to who she wants to gather information from.

> FG Expert: "We began with you wanting to know why students do not return after their first year, but you now realize that it's practically impossible to get the ones who left to talk to us. So, now we want to know why students return after their first year. Who do you want to get information from? Who can have a discussion of 60 to 90 minutes related to the research question?"

> Shirley: "I would like to hear multiple perspectives from students, faculty, and staff."

> FG Expert: "Okay . . . if you want to hear from current students, which students? Those who returned who were in academic difficulty? Or those who returned who were academically successful?"

Shirley: "I think we want to hear from both so we can compare what they say. The ones who returned who were in difficulty are probably somewhat similar to those who did not return."

FG Expert: "And you mentioned gathering information from faculty. Who do you mean? Tenured faculty, tenure track, non–tenure track? How about those who teach lower-division general education courses versus upper-division major courses?"

Shirley: "Hmm . . . so many decisions. Why can't we just conduct one group of students, one group of faculty, and one group of staff?"

FG Expert: "Typically focus groups are conducted with homogeneous groups of people. Would you expect students who returned in academic difficulty to respond differently than those who returned in academic success? Similarly, would you expect tenured and tenure-track faculty to have different responses? What about staff who work directly with students versus senior administrators who do not have as much contact with students?"

Shirley: "Okay, I can see that there may be differences between students in academic difficulty versus those who were successful. However, I would not expect differences between tenured and tenure-track faculty."

FG Expert: "Perhaps not, but how comfortable would tenure-track faculty feel discussing this topic with tenured faculty who will participate in their tenure decision?"

Shirley: "I can see where that might be a concern for some topics, but I don't think that will be a problem with this topic. And, we can make sure they are not in groups with faculty in their department or college. I would be more interested in hearing from the lower-division general education faculty who teach these students versus those who only teach the upper-division major courses, however."

FG Expert: "Good idea. What about staff? Which staff members would be able to address the research questions? Those who advise students or teach college success or orientation courses or senior administrators?"

Shirley: "For now, let's focus on frontline staff who have a lot of student contact in residence life, advising, career counseling, student support services, and so on."

FG Expert: "Would you expect to hear any differences between men and women or among different races or ethnicities?"

Shirley: "No, I don't think so."

During our conversation with Shirley, we have to make sure the segments are representative of the population and able to provide meaningful information that addresses the scope of the project. If Shirley really wants to hear from all of the groups mentioned, then the project becomes very large.

FG Expert: "If you want to gather information from all of these populations, then the project is going to expand. We need at least 2 to 3 focus groups per segment of the population, with 7 to 10 participants per focus group."

Shirley: "Whoa, why do we need multiple groups for each segment?"

FG Expert: "Because we want to make sure that all of the data are accurate. When we get two or three groups from each segment saying approximately the same things, we can be more confident that the data are accurate."

Discussion then moves to when she would like to have the information. Determining when the report is needed helps sketch the time line of when the focus groups will be conducted. During the conversation we need to think about what is ideal and what is "doable."

FG Expert: "When would you like this information? Is there a presentation you are going to make to a committee? Or some deadline for a decision based on these data? We need to know the due date in order to reverse schedule the planning."

Resources, such as time, money, and staff, need to be considered when developing a focus group project.

FG Expert: "What is the budget for this project? We need to factor in catering costs, as well as incentives for participants and moderators."

These last two questions should be addressed before finalizing decisions about the populations. Clarifying the time line and the resources needed is critical, as these realities may impact which populations and how many segments will be included. Clients often begin wanting to hear from everyone; as they work with the FG Expert and realize the resources required, they sharpen their purpose and research questions. While these early conversations can be challenging, they result in a significantly improved project with a clearly defined scope of work. As a result, the Final Report will generally provide more explicit and accurate answers to the research questions.

Focus Group Population and Segments

The project topic, purpose statement, and research questions determine if gathering data from multiple populations or segments is necessary. Remember that a population is a collection of people who share some common characteristic. Within this collection of people there can be segments who might be expected to have differing attitudes and opinions. Some focus group topics need input from multiple populations or segments. Broad topics, such as academic success, can have input from faculty teaching undergraduate students, academic advisers, and students themselves plus segments of each of these populations. The implications of including more than one population or segment are significant.

Higher education institutions contain many populations to draw on— teaching and research faculty, administrators, staff, and students. Each of those populations also includes multiple segments that differ based on the population. Consider students: There are graduate and undergraduate students; undergraduate students in a particular year of college (first, second, third, or fourth year); African American, White, and students of other race and ethnicities; part-time and full-time students; and combinations of those characteristics and more. With respect to teaching faculty there are tenure-track, tenured, and non–tenure-track faculty; further, there may be full professors, instructors, adjuncts, or graduate students who teach primarily first-year students, upper-division majors, or graduate students; race and gender may be important differentiators as well. Will tenured faculty have a different outlook on a topic than tenure-track or non–tenure-track faculty? Will undergraduate students have different viewpoints than graduate students about the topic? Even within these segments, there can be more discrete segments. These segments might be demographic (e.g., gender, race, ethnicity, and citizenship) or experiential (e.g., first-year students versus seniors; faculty teaching lower-division, prerequisite courses versus those teaching senior seminar or capstone courses).

Each of these segments of the population has a different job from the others, is positioned differently within the structure of the institution, and confronts different evaluation expectations, and so likely has different experiences with most topics. Thus, considerable thought needs to go into which populations and segments can and should respond to the focus group purpose and research questions. Clarifying the population and segments ensures that the participants are likely to know enough about or have sufficient experience with the topic so they can answer the focus group questions in depth and with thoughtfulness. In short, they must be able to have a useful discussion of 60 to 90 minutes about the project topic.

The project topic will dictate the population and segments of the population. For instance, if Shirley wants to know about undergraduate students' sense of belonging, it may be beneficial to hear from underrepresented students as a separate group so we can learn about their common experiences. Is there evidence to support separating the groups by gender? Will participants feel free to share their opinions within the group or will they feel stifled based on the composition of the group? How comfortable will tenure-track faculty feel participating in a focus group with tenured faculty? Do institutional data reveal differences in segments of the population (e.g., female students are more academically successful than males; female faculty are more likely to get stuck at the associate professor level than males)?

Population Segments and Sampling

Remember that the purpose of focus groups is to explore a topic in depth. To do this well, the participants should have common experiences that lead to deep discussions, a goal that is more likely to be reached using purposeful sampling methods (Krueger & Casey, 2015; Morgan, 1988). Purposeful sampling—also known as purposive, judgmental, selective, or subjective sampling—is a method that relies on the judgment of the researcher to identify the population characteristics that are likely to make a difference in the findings. Compatibility in terms of the purpose of the focus group emerges as the most important consideration when selecting participants. Morgan (1997) notes that "right group composition will generate free-flowing discussions that contain useful data" (p. 55), and Morgan and Scannell (1998) state that "compatibility on shared experiences often matters more than demographic characteristics" (p. 61). Compatibility is most likely to occur when a group's participants are homogeneous in ways that the client and FG Expert have judged to matter for the purpose of the focus group. Participants of compatible groups perceive that they have similar experiences and backgrounds as other members and so do not need to define or explain their comments to one another.

Number of Participants

Ultimately each segment should include 2 to 3 focus groups, each of which will comprise 7 to 10 participants per group who possess some shared quality that matters with respect to the topic,—that is, a group that is homogeneous. Two to 3 focus groups per segment are needed to express confidence that the themes that arise from a group are similar across all groups; this increases confidence in the accuracy of the data. If we conducted only 1 focus group, we would not know how representative it is of the segment. Thus, identifying multiple segments dramatically expands the number of focus groups that should be conducted.

Since focus groups should be like a "lively conversation between neighbors" (Morgan, 1988, p. 22), each group needs 7 to 10 participants. Fewer than 7 could slow the conversation, and more than 10 could create an environment where participants are talking over each other or struggling to share their thoughts. However, the client and FG Expert will often have knowledge that makes smaller or larger groups useful. Smaller groups are possible when the topic is "hot" or when the participants are likely to know each other. For example, a group of 4 vice presidents will probably be engaged, and the conversation will flow easily. On the downside, participants who are members of established groups may fall into regular patterns of interaction that interrupt thoughtful consideration of the actual topic. In contrast, first-year students may be shy and insecure among one another, making larger groups desirable.

As can be seen, identifying the populations, segments, and number of participants per group has important consequences for the time line, budget, and findings. Consider a project that requires information from tenured, tenure-track, and non-tenure-track faculty. In order to gather enough information from the segments to be able to draw meaningful conclusions, 2 to 3 focus groups with each segment should be conducted, totaling 63 to 90 participants as follows: 3 tenured groups + 3 tenure-track groups + 3 non-tenure-track focus groups, with 7 to 10 faculty members per group = 63 to 90 participants needed. And that presumes that the topic is not likely to be race, gender, or discipline specific!

In our example, Shirley wants to gather information from three populations: students, faculty, and staff. Each of those populations has multiple segments, and decisions must be made as to which segments matter for the research purpose, such as first-year students, tenured faculty who teach intro courses, and advisers. Gathering information from all three populations and their segments will dramatically increase the scope, size, and cost of the project, as well as lengthen the time it takes to gather and report the data. After delineating the number of groups that need to be conducted and participants needed, the conversation with Shirley should focus on what is ideal and what is "doable."

Working with Shirley we have purposively selected the segments of each population who we believe can best answer our research questions (sophomores who returned in academic difficulty, sophomores who returned in academic success, tenured faculty who teach intro courses, and advisers). These populations and segments were carefully and deliberately (purposively) chosen rather than randomly selected. However, purposively choosing individual participants may be difficult if we do not know many of the members of a segment or if the segment is large. So, we randomly select potential student participants from within each student segment and invite them to participate. With smaller groups of people we know, like tenured faculty or the advisers who work directly with students, we might be better able to purposively sample them because we know who will give us good, unbiased data and who may try to dominate the group or lead it toward a (their) predetermined conclusion.

Participation

Ensuring participation—actually getting people to show up and engage with the questions—emerges as one of the most important and challenging parts of conducting a focus group. From incentives to time and location to multiple reminders, resources must be dedicated to ensuring participation. Without an investment of time and funds, the project will not attract a sufficient number of participants to ensure a good conversation of 60 to 90 minutes to yield meaningful information to make decisions.

Attracting participation begins with choosing a compelling topic. We continuously ask Shirley, "Will this topic encourage participation in a discussion of 60 to 90 minutes among the participants we have chosen?" If there is any hesitation or concern about this, it is important to review the Research Proposal and confirm that this is the right topic, that these are the right segments, and that focus groups are the appropriate methodology.

James Vignette (Access)

Recall that James chose to investigate one of three potential topics in chapter 3: How do we encourage students from underrepresented groups to enroll at the institution? James and his committee also developed some research questions:

- How important is it for students from underrepresented groups to attend college? This college?
- How important is it for their families?
- What worries students from underrepresented groups about attending college? This college?
- What can the faculty and staff do to help students from underrepresented groups to be successful both academically and socially at this college?
- What are the chances students from underrepresented groups will be successful in this college?

At the end of their last conversation, the FG Expert gave James and his committee an assignment: to begin thinking about what populations of students they wanted to have in their focus groups and how best to recruit them.

Do they want to talk to first-year students who have just begun their college courses or students who have been on campus for two or three years? Do they want to talk only to students from underrepresented groups or would they like to talk to a variety of students for comparison? Should these focus groups be separated by race or gender? That is, is there a problem with working with men and women of different racial or ethnic backgrounds in the same focus groups? Or would we expect to hear different things from students from different backgrounds? Are there any other critical factors or characteristics that should be included?

> FG Expert: "How is your Research Proposal coming, James? Have you and your committee made any decisions about what populations of students to invite to the focus groups?"

> James: "We have some thoughts to share with you and get your advice. I think we want to talk to both first-year students from underrepresented groups and students in their junior year to see what each might identify as concerns and make recommendations for improving the situation for underrepresented students. I do not think that we need majority group students for comparison. We have a fairly good idea of their concerns. What do you think? How many focus groups will we need to conduct?"

> FG Expert: "Good thoughts, James. I think it is good to talk to first-year students who are still experiencing the transition to college and to juniors who have had some opportunity to reflect on their transition to college. While it might be good to have a comparison with majority students, I agree that that is not necessary now."

> James: "So how many groups do we need? Two groups for first-year students and two groups for junior students?"

> FG Expert: "That would be the case unless there are any other demographic characteristics that you think might affect the discussion and results."

> James: "No, I do not see any reason to have separate groups for gender and race or ethnicity; do you?"

> FG Expert: "No, that makes sense to me. We usually recommend two to three groups so two each (four groups in total) would be the minimum. If we hear similar themes we will feel comfortable with two groups of each. However, if we hear significantly different themes from a group in either constituency, we may need to conduct another group with that constituency. Now what is your plan for identifying and recruiting these students?"

The conversation continues with James explaining how they will identify and draw the population from the institution's student information system. The FG Expert talks about sampling procedures and sample sizes to answer the question: How many students do we have to invite in order to get how many to respond in order to get how many to actually attend the focus group? The answer requires both knowledge of sampling procedures and knowledge about the responsiveness of students from underrepresented groups. Perhaps James knows this or perhaps they have to consult someone else who works with students from underrepresented groups. They also discuss how best to recruit these students and appropriate incentives. At the end of their conversation, the FG Expert asks James to work with his group to turn their research questions into focus group topic questions. The FG Expert also asks them to develop some ideas for closed-ended warm-up and wrap-up questions.

The sampling plan is fully described in the full Research Proposal in Appendix C.

Chris Vignette (Affordability)

Recall that the FG Expert tasked the committee to draft their Research Proposal, including their research questions, sample focus group topic questions, and a plan for identifying the populations of participants. The committee's draft research questions are (a) What is the impact of working on student success while earning a college degree?; (b) Other than earning money, what is the benefit of working while attending college?; and (c) Is there a difference depending on whether students work on or off campus and how many hours per week they work? Following are their revised focus group topic questions:

- What is the value of a college education to you? To your family?
- To what extent were college costs (tuition, fees, room and board, books and supplies, etc.) a factor in deciding to attend or remain in college? To remain at this college?
- To what extent does working have an impact on your ability to be successful academically?
- What is the benefit of working while attending college, beyond simply earning money?
- What is the impact of working on campus on your academic success? What about working off campus? What is the impact of working more than 20 hours per week versus working 20 or fewer hours per week?

FG Expert: "I like the edits to your topic questions, but before we do much more editing, it will be helpful to know what populations you plan to invite to your focus groups—undergraduate or graduate students? Faculty? Staff?"

Chris: "We have not thought much about inviting graduate students but did not even consider faculty or staff. Why would we include them?"

FG Expert: "You certainly do not need to invite faculty or staff, especially if they are not in a position to address your research question. Do faculty teaching students who work have a perspective to add? Do staff supervising students working on campus have a perspective to add?"

Chris: "Hmm . . . good questions. We will have to think about faculty and staff. But let's talk about undergraduate versus graduate students first. Our greatest concern is about undergraduate students, especially first- and second-year undergraduates. They seem to us to be the most vulnerable. Third- and fourth-year undergraduates have been successful for at least half of their college careers as students, and graduate students have completed bachelor's degrees, so they would seem to have the ability to manage work and school. And, for many graduate students, work in the form of assistant-ships is part of the expectation."

FG Expert: "Good thoughts, Chris. Lower- and upper-division under-graduate students and graduate students will likely all have different per-spectives. And graduate assistants have different methods of funding their educations. To what extent is it important to talk to each? As it stands, your research questions suggest only undergraduates."

The conversation continues for the remainder of the meeting, and the FG Expert asks the committee to make some decisions before the next meeting. The FG Expert also tells them that choosing multiple populations can greatly increase the number of focus groups that need to be offered, which will also increase the cost and time needed to complete the project. Few decisions about conducting focus groups can be made independently of other issues—this is not a linear process but instead resembles a spiral in which we cycle forward and backward through the steps of the proposal. Decisions made or challenges encountered in some of the later steps may cause us to reevaluate decisions made about steps earlier in the process. The FG Expert asks the committee to begin drafting the Moderator's Guide, including warm-up and wrap-up questions along with their draft topic questions for the next meeting.

The Research Proposal with sampling plan for this vignette is in Appendix D.

5

STEP #3: DESIGN THE MODERATOR'S GUIDE

A Cookbook Approach

Rigorous and relevant focus groups result from a complete and well-considered Moderator's Guide that is built from the Research Proposal.

FG Expert: "Hi, Shirley. Now that we have specific research questions and populations and segments to focus on, we need to construct the Moderator's Guides for the different segments."

Shirley: "One Moderator's Guide won't suffice?"

FG Expert: "Typically not. Would the questions you ask students make sense to faculty and staff? Or vice versa? However, we may or may not need separate Moderator's Guides for faculty and staff. So, let's start with two separate Moderator's Guides, one for students and one for faculty and staff, and see how well they fit all segments. We have a template to help us with this."

Shirley: "How should we proceed?"

FG Expert: "First, use the template we have developed and focus on the topic questions to be included in the Moderator's Guide. I will e-mail you the template. Second, use the research questions in the proposal to develop those topic questions. Edit them as needed to make them more conversational so the participants can answer them. Make sure they are open-ended questions that will encourage discussion. Add prompts or follow-up questions. The prompts may or may not be required by the moderators to stimulate conversation or clarify a particular point."

Shirley: "OK, I think we can do that. What do you mean by prompts that may or may not be required?"

FG Expert: "Prompts are statements that help jump-start the conversation when participants seem stuck. Sometimes we include prompts that are just there for the moderators should participants have some difficulty beginning their discussion or if there is confusion about what is being asked. For example, when you ask a question about resources, you may want to have a list of existing resources that the moderators can use as needed to prompt discussion. Conversely, you may want to make sure that some prompts are actually asked of each group. For example, among the resources you list you may have included tutoring, and you really want to know what students are saying about tutoring; so, you provide a prompt for the moderators to make sure they ask about tutoring if students do not mention it."

Shirley: "Hmm . . . it might be interesting to see if anyone mentions tutoring without prompting them."

FG Expert: "Indeed, sometimes what is not said is as important as what is said, especially since we have been promoting our tutoring program so much recently. And it might be interesting to see the differences between students who returned in academic difficulty and those who returned academically successful. That is an important finding."

Shirley: "And we need to know that. I think we can do this."

FG Expert: "I know that you and your committee can do this, Shirley. The important thing for now is to get a complete first draft. We typically go through five or six drafts of a Moderator's Guide until we have one with which we are satisfied. Then we share it with the moderators, and they always do a nice job of fine-tuning it or telling us where we missed the mark, so we do one more final draft. The Moderator's Guide along with the moderators are critical to collecting consistent and accurate data."

Purpose of the Moderator's Guide

The Moderator's Guide is a highly structured instrument that all moderators follow as they conduct their particular focus groups. The Moderator's Guide ensures the consistency and accuracy of the focus group methodology because it serves as a guidebook or road map for moderators. Remember that Step 1 requires the careful construction of the Research Proposal that identifies the project's purpose and research questions. The Research Proposal process both ensures the accuracy of the focus groups and contributes to the building of the

Moderator's Guide. An excellent Moderator's Guide is a script that contains opening and closing statements about the purpose of the focus group, the specific questions to be asked in an order that encourages a fluid conversation, and the prompts the moderators are to use. Drafts are reviewed by the client, stakeholders (others who want the research), and moderators for feedback, clarification, and validation prior to the first focus group. A detailed Moderator's Guide ensures consistency because all groups cover the same topics since they are asked the same questions in the same manner and order. Then, upon completion of the focus groups, the moderators use the guide as an outline for their report. This chapter explains the purpose and content of the Moderator's Guide, along with how to construct it using the template developed by the ODU Team and tested with more than 100 focus groups over 20 years.

Creating the Moderator's Guide

Creating and finalizing the Moderator's Guide involves two basic steps that are carried out over the phone, by e-mail, or in person depending on the situation and stage in the process: first, developing the questions, and second, reviewing and finalizing the Moderator's Guide with the client, stakeholders, and moderators. The ODU Team takes a cookbook approach to both completing and using the Moderator's Guide. We have a standard template that helps clients work on the first draft.

Of course, Moderator's Guides go through a few drafts as they are discussed among the FG Expert and the client. Once everyone feels confident about the guide, they present it to the stakeholders and moderators for their feedback. We recommend that the meeting with the client and stakeholders be conducted in person with everyone present. While e-mail is fine for soliciting initial feedback either individually or in groups, there is no substitute for getting people together to make certain that everyone actually closely considers the guide, as well as to identify and correct possible missteps or confusions. By meeting to discuss the guide, important conversations about the meaning of a question or word occur. The purpose at this point is to ascertain that all questions are relevant to the project's purpose, address the research questions, are likely to make sense to and engage the participants, and will yield useful data.

For example, the phrasing of a question about students' library use may sound fine to someone who is a faculty member with his or her own ideas about the purpose of the library, while another person who is a librarian may know that students use the library very differently than their professors. It is critical that confusions be identified and corrected early on so that the focus groups yield useful data.

Content of the Moderator's Guide

The Moderator's Guide has five main parts:

1. Introduction to the focus group
   a. Welcome and introduction of the focus group purpose and moderators
   b. Explanation of the group process and guidelines
   c. Explanation of audio recording and equipment
   d. Transition to begin group
2. Introduction of participants
3. Warm-up question
4. Topic and questions for discussions
5. Wrap-up question and closing the focus group

A template for the Moderator's Guide is found in Appendix G, and Appendices H through K contain several examples of Moderator's Guides that accompany the three vignettes.

The Introduction to and Closing of the Focus Group

Parts 1, 2, some of 5, the introduction, and the closing of the focus group, are standard. However, their importance is critical, so they must not be treated in a cavalier manner.

The focus group begins with a clear statement of purpose derived from the Research Proposal. For instance, the purpose statement for Shirley's project on retention of first-year students, as proposed in Step 1, is:

"The purpose of this focus group is to
- learn from students why they decide to return to the institution (Population: Students);
- obtain student perceptions of the challenges of the undergraduate experience at the institution; (Population: Students) and
- determine what resources students need to help them be successful" (Populations: Students, Faculty, Advisers).

The focus group always begins with: "The purpose of this focus group is to . . ." Here are some examples:

- "The purpose of this focus group is to:
  o inform the university's strategic planning process by exploring (a) the strengths and weaknesses of the university, and (b) the

opportunities and challenges that exist in our environment (Populations: Faculty, Staff, Administrators, Students);

o generate interest in, and possible topics for, a plan to enhance student learning at the university (Population: Faculty);

o help determine guidelines for graduate program administration. The primary purpose is to develop a job description for the job of graduate program director (GPD) and to figure out which duties of graduate program administration properly belong to the GPD and which belong to other entities in the department, college, or university (Population: GPDs);

o identify knowledge, skills, abilities, and attitudes of successful physical therapists (PTs) and assess how well the university physical therapy program prepares graduates to be successful practitioners (Population: PT Employers);

o explore (a) how the university is viewed by folks outside of the university, and (b) what kinds of things we need to do to attract more people to campus" (Population: External Constituencies, that is, community members not affiliated with the university).

Note how aligning the purpose statement with the population makes it clear that in some projects, such as Shirley's, different Moderator's Guides are required.

Moderator introductions follow and include the moderators' names and a statement of their responsibilities:

- "My name is _____ and this is _____. Our job is to facilitate your discussion, record your responses, and keep time to make sure that we cover all of the topics."

The following are the group guidelines. One of the moderators relates the guidelines to participants slowly and in the moderator's own words. All issues should be covered:

1. Moderators should speak less than one-third of the time.
2. While one moderator facilitates the discussion, the other will be taking notes for analysis, BUT NO NAMES will be recorded.
3. Respect the confidentiality of each participant by not quoting or attributing comments to anyone outside of the group.
4. Everyone should participate.
5. Discussion and disagreement are encouraged; no need to reach consensus.

6. There are no right or wrong opinions; just different points of view.
7. Only one person should speak at a time—no side conversations.
8. Please be open and honest about your attitudes, opinions, and experiences —we want to hear it all.

If the focus group is to be audiotaped, the moderators then provide an explanation of the recording and the equipment:

"The focus group is being audio recorded today for data analyses. We assure you that:

1. ***ONLY*** the Research Team will have access to the recordings;
2. the recordings will be used ***ONLY*** for data analyses; and
3. ***ONLY*** group results will be reported, and no individuals will be identified; however, we may use some direct quotations to emphasize a particular point.
4. ***Confidentiality***: Please keep confidential all information that others share with the group when you leave."

The last piece of the introduction to the group is the transition statement, "If there are no questions or concerns, let's begin." This is voiced as a statement, not a question. Moderators should not allow the participants to spend any time discussing or debating the guidelines, since that will detract from the main topic of discussion. The moderators must establish that these guidelines are nonnegotiable; they don't actually make that statement, but it is implied in the transition statement.

The second part of the Moderator's Guide, introduction of participants, marks the shift into the start of the focus group. The moderator asks participants to state their first names and any other specific information that may be relevant to the purpose of the focus group; only information that is relevant to the purpose of the group should be requested. This may include the following:

- For faculty and staff: department, number of years at the university
- For students: class standing, major
- For community members: occupation, relationship to the university, if any

Finally, a portion of part 5 of the Moderator's Guide—closing of the focus group—is a very simple "thank you" to the participants and dismissal.

Parts 3, 4, and some of 5 of the Moderator's Guide contain the questions for discussion, the substance of the focus groups.

Developing Questions

Clarifying the topic and writing questions for the participants to discuss is key to successful focus groups. Remember that the Research Proposal clearly lists the purpose, topics, research questions, and populations for the focus groups. In this way the Research Proposal guides the development of the specific questions to be discussed during the group. Indeed, often at least some of the questions to be asked during the group arise as the proposal is developed, and a few may even come out of the "I want to do a focus group" call. Eventually, each question to be discussed during the focus group should come from or be clearly linked to one of the topics and its research questions.

Finalizing the questions to be discussed occurs in several stages. The early stages should be treated as brainstorming sessions with the FG Expert, client, and stakeholders all writing out as many questions as possible. The only "rule" that question writers need at this point is to aim for open-ended questions that are relatively short but broad enough to elicit discussion, easy to understand, engaging, and can help answer the research questions.

The initial question writing may be done individually, with all contributors submitting questions within a defined time period (e.g., one week), or it may be done as a group in a single work session. The former is easy as the only scheduling involves a due date, while the latter often elicits better questions as well as engages the group in the process. Everyone is busy and meetings are sometimes hard to schedule, but then so is time to work on a project individually. To the extent possible, bringing people together in this early brainstorming session of initial question writing usually results in better questions and a more energized group process and is a relief because the work gets done and is not hanging on as a reminder on everyone's calendar.

Next, the FG Expert reviews all questions to identify similar themes and question styles and to consider whether the questions are appropriate. The issue of the appropriateness of questions refers to consistency and accuracy. Questions should be open-ended and likely to engage participants and generate discussion. This is most likely if the questions are relatively short and easy to understand.

Most focus groups cover 4 to 5 topics related to the research questions. This results in 4 to 8 questions for a group session of 60 to 90 minutes. The questions should be arranged in a flow that will seem logical to participants and move from general to more specific questions if possible. Questions that participants might find somewhat sensitive should be placed in the middle.

Based on the research questions presented in Step 1, Shirley and her committee developed the following questions for their student focus groups (see Appendix H):

1. What are some reasons that you chose to return to the university for a second year?
2. What are some reasons other students you know did not return?
3. Please tell us about the quality of your undergraduate experience here.
   a. your academic experiences both in and out of class
   b. your social experiences in the campus community
4. What did you find most challenging about your academic experience?
5. If you were to redo your first semester here, what would you do differently?
6. What resources did you use for assistance with academics? What resources did you use to help you become a member of the university community? What additional resources do students need to help them be successful? [If students struggle identifying resources OR if you want to ask about a couple of specific resources, list them here.]
7. What recommendations do you have for the incoming class of first-year students?
8. What recommendations do you have for the faculty and administrators who will work with them?

Following are other examples of focus group questions:

Focus group questions for the university's strategic plan:

- What are the strengths of the university?
- If you were to invest in three strengths with an eye to ensuring the future success of the university, what would they be?
- What are the weaknesses of the university?
- Are there any weaknesses it would be very important to correct in order to move the university forward in a positive manner?
- Are there any things that the university is doing that should be eliminated to make the institution stronger?
- Are there any obstacles or barriers in the external environment that you see that would prevent the university from accomplishing its goals? Is there anything the university should undertake to respond to what you see as opportunities in the environment now or in the future?

Focus group questions for the student learning initiative:

- In which areas of student learning are our students or graduates performing relatively well?
- In which areas of student learning do you think our students and graduates need to improve?
- Why do you think students are not doing well in these areas?
- What can the university do to change this?

Focus group questions regarding graduate program administration:

- What duties do you think definitely belong under the GPD's responsibility?
- What duties definitely belong to other personnel in the department, dean's office, or graduate school?
- Are there any other duties or responsibilities for graduate administration that we have not identified?
- Given the variety of programs and varying levels of support for GPDs, what resources do GPDs most need to do their jobs well?
- What additional suggestions do you have as the GPD job description is refined?

Focus group questions about a physical therapy program:

- What knowledge, skills, abilities, and attitudes or values characterize successful PTs?
- To what extent do university physical therapy graduates have the following qualities to successfully practice physical therapy? (The qualities listed are handed to participants or may be written on a whiteboard that has been previously covered up.):
  o display knowledge base
  o demonstrate skills and abilities
  o display the appropriate attitudes and values
  o communicate effectively with the patient, family or caregivers, health care team, and the general public
  o demonstrate effective clinical problem-solving skills
  o demonstrate effective time-management skills
  o utilize evidence to guide practice
  o engage in professional development and demonstrate an interest in lifelong learning
- What are specific areas of strengths that seem to reoccur?

- What are specific areas of weakness that seem to reoccur?
- What can the university physical therapy program do to improve the curriculum or teaching methods?

Focus group questions for external constituencies to learn their view of the university:

- What do people in the community think or say about the university?
- In order to serve the community, ideally what should the university do or be?
- Are there any activities or educational programs that the university should add or subtract?
- What aspects of the physical campus do you like or would you change?
- What are your impressions of the educational experience at the university compared to other institutions?
- What do others say about the educational experience at the university compared to other institutions?
- Would you attend or would you encourage family members or friends to attend the university? Why or why not?
- What value and contributions does the university make to the community?
- What are the best features of the university? If you were marketing the university what would you say about it?
- What are the worst features of the university? What should we be doing better?

It is also important to seriously consider how different populations and segments of the population might respond differently to the questions. If it is anticipated that they will, then different segments will require separate focus groups, and so different Moderator's Guides may be needed.

For example, after developing the questions for student focus groups, Shirley and her committee quickly realized that the questions would not be appropriate questions to ask faculty or staff. To start, they reviewed the purpose statements and found them relevant to faculty and administrators as well as students. Therefore, they proceeded to develop the following questions for their faculty and staff groups. Note that these track the questions asked of students but are worded in a way appropriate for faculty and staff. (See Appendix I.)

1. What do you think causes some students to not return to the university for their second year?
2. Why is it that other students choose to return to the university?

3. What are some characteristics of our undergraduate experience that help students to be successful
    a. academically, both in and out of class?
    b. socially in becoming part of the campus community?
4. What is it that you think students find most challenging
    a. academically, both in and out of class?
    b. socially in becoming part of the campus community?
5. What resources do we offer to students in need of assistance with academics or with becoming a member of the university community? What additional resources do students need to help them be successful?
    [If faculty and administrators struggle identifying resources OR if you want to ask about a couple of specific resources list them here.]
6. What recommendations do you have for improving the success of the incoming class of first-year students?

After reviewing these questions, Shirley and her committee decided that they would work well for both faculty and staff, so although the two populations would be in separate focus groups, the same Moderator's Guide could be used for each population.

The Warm-Up and Wrap-Up Questions

The warm-up question opens the conversation, focuses attention on the topic, and gets people ready to start talking. It is one short-answer question that is related to the topic and to which participants write their answer on a five-inch-by-eight-inch note card. Writing on the cards is not necessarily a requirement, but it is our preference for the reasons stated. The note cards also serve as data for the moderator's report. Some examples of warm-up questions include:

- In a word, phrase, or sentence, describe your image of the university.
- What are one or two of the most important things you expect students to learn in college?
- What is the one duty of the GPD that you find most rewarding?
- When you hire a PT, other than having graduated from an accredited program, what is the most important qualification you consider?
- Describe the university in a word, phrase, or sentence.
    o Describe the university in a word, phrase, or sentence as you think others see it. (This project used this second warm-up question that was written on a different color five-inch-by-eight-inch note card.)

Shirley and her committee decided to ask students, "What is the most memorable (or surprising) thing about your first year at the university?" Faculty and advisers were asked, "What is something unique that you noticed about last year's first-year students?"

The wrap-up question stops the conversation by asking everyone to write down one final thought about the topic on another five-inch-by-eight-inch note card of a different color than the first. The different color allows for easy sorting of the two questions. Having participants write the answer stops the conversation and closes the group. Following are sample wrap-up questions:

- If you had to choose one student learning outcome in which you would like to invest over the next five years, what would it be?
- What is the one most important suggestion you have for improving the position of GPD?
- If you had one recommendation for the university physical therapy program, what would it be?
- If you had one piece of advice for the university president, what would it be?

Shirley and her committee liked the idea of following up the last question that asked participants to brainstorm recommendations with the challenge to narrow their recommendations to just one: "If you had one suggestion for the student success committee, what would it be?" They thought this would work well for both students and faculty and staff.

Closing the Focus Group

As individuals finish writing their answers to the wrap-up question, the moderators take the note cards from them and thank them for coming. The moderators may stand up during this process, which acts as a signal to participants that it is time to leave. Along with the wrap-up question, this action of standing and accepting the note cards closes the focus group itself, which may be difficult to do otherwise with particularly provocative topics of grave concern to participants. Never end a group with another open-ended question such as, "Does anyone have anything else to add before we finish?" A question like this can reopen any or all of the topics previously discussed that have already been thoroughly discussed and closed.

Copies of the Moderator's Guide for Shirley's first-year student success project are in Appendices H and I.

Review the Moderator's Guide

Once a draft version of the Moderator's Guide is completed, a meeting is scheduled with the client and stakeholders. (The moderators review the guide during their training.) Since they asked for the focus groups to be conducted, the client and stakeholders will tell the experts whether or not the content they think is important has been covered. They can also assess the extent to which they think these topic questions are well phrased to answer their research questions. The purpose of the meeting is to obtain feedback to ascertain that the questions are relevant to the purpose, are likely to make sense to and engage participants, and will yield useful data. During the meeting, the FG Expert, client, and stakeholders review and discuss the questions while keeping the population and segments explicitly in mind, again asking themselves and one another a series of questions about each question:

- Is this question relevant to the purpose of the focus group?
- Will the participants understand the question?
- Will they want to discuss the issues raised in the question?
- Is it likely that what they say during the discussion will help the Team answer the research question?

Summary

The Moderator's Guide is critical for ensuring consistency in the process of data collection because it serves as a guidebook for the moderators. The Moderator's Guide includes everything the moderators need to know to conduct the focus group and much of what they need to say during it. The substantive content is created using the Research Proposal, and a template is provided to make getting started easy. The Moderator's Guide is reviewed with the FG Expert, client, stakeholders, and later the moderators to ensure that the questions to be discussed will elicit data that get at the purpose of the focus group, and that participants are able to answer and interested in answering. The Moderator's Guide then serves as the outline for moderators to use as they write up their report (which will be discussed in chapter 8).

Of course, the Moderator's Guide is dependent on the moderators themselves. Thus, the next chapter discusses how to select and train the moderators.

James Vignette (Access)

Recall that after agreeing on the populations from which to select their focus group participants, the FG Expert asked James and his committee to begin drafting some focus group topic questions and prompts for the Moderator's Guide based on their research questions. The FG Expert also asked them to draft warm-up and wrap-up questions along with guidelines for the focus group conversation. The FG Expert directed James that they were welcome to adopt and adapt the guidelines in our Moderator's Guide template (Appendix G). For the warm-up question, the FG Expert encouraged James and his committee to give some thought to a question that is related to the topic but easy to answer and nonthreatening. What is a good warm-up question to ask underrepresented students that they will feel comfortable answering? How about, "When you think of the university, what is the first thought that comes into your mind?" Or, "What are three or four words you would use to describe your experiences at the university thus far?" Or, "What is one experience that has helped you to transition from high school to the university?" The FG Expert will work with James and his committee to edit these questions as needed to facilitate the conversation among participants. They will draft any prompts that might serve as follow-up questions or will help the moderators to keep the conversation going if it drags a bit.

James: "I hope that you received the draft Moderator's Guide that I e-mailed to you and had time to review it before our meeting today."

FG Expert: "I did and I think it is a very good first draft. Not to worry, as I mentioned we usually work through five or six drafts of Moderator's Guides before we are ready to use them. Let's start at the beginning and work our way through your draft. I see that you adopted our usual guidelines, which is good. What about the warm-up question?"

James: "We thought we would ask them to rate their experience transitioning from high school to the institution. What do you think?"

FG Expert: "That sounds like a potentially good topic question, James, but it may be a bit intimidating as a warm-up question. How about something like, 'When I say the institution, what is the first thing that comes to your mind?' or 'Please list three to five words you would use to describe the institution.'"

James: "Both of those sound good. Let's use the first one, 'When I say the institution, what is the first thing that comes to mind?' And I believe that you said we can ask students to write their thoughts on five-inch-by-eight-inch cards as well as discuss them."

FG Expert: "Asking them to write their warm-up thoughts gives us some good, accurate data to analyze. In addition, having it on individual five-inch-by-eight-inch cards allows us to more quickly sort the cards into thematic piles."

James: "Great. What about our topic questions?"

FG Expert: "Okay, let's look at the first topic question, 'How important is it for you to attend college? This college?' Let's separate those two questions and use 'this college?' as a follow-up prompt. I think we want to hear their answers to the first question first. However, I can see that their answers to the second question are important as well. Are there other prompts we could include in case the moderators need some help getting participants talking? Or are there other follow-up prompts that you would like to ask?"

This conversation between the FG Expert and James continues until they have reviewed and edited all of the topics and their prompts as well as the warm-up and wrap-up questions. Later in the discussion, the FG Expert asks James to give some thought to selecting the moderators. While James and members of his committee cannot moderate these focus groups, they can participate in training for future focus group projects. Beyond that, do they want to select other faculty and administrators or perhaps graduate students? How important is it to have members of underrepresented groups as at least one co-moderator in each group? James agrees to take these questions to his committee. The FG Expert offers James a copy of the list of trained moderators at the university.

There is a copy of the Moderator's Guide for this project in Appendix J.

Chris Vignette (Affordability)

Recall that the FG Expert asked the committee to make some decisions about which populations to include—lower-division undergraduates, upper-division undergraduates, graduate students, faculty, or staff. The FG Expert also reminded them that simply choosing all of these would require a significant number of focus groups. It is critical to know which populations will be invited to participate in order to determine whether or not separate Moderator's Guides will be required. While we might use the same Moderator's Guide for all undergraduate students, we would likely need a slightly different one for faculty and staff.

FG Expert: "Our plan today is to begin looking at your topic questions for the focus groups along with the warm-up and wrap-up questions you have developed. But first we need to decide what populations you want to invite to your focus groups."

Chris: "We had much discussion about the populations and good points were made about conducting focus groups with all of them. However, considering the budget and resources that would be required, we decided to begin with first- and second-year and third- and fourth-year undergraduates for now. What do you think?"

FG Expert: "That sounds fine to me and also feasible considering obvious budget issues. They also seem to be the populations of greatest concern. That means that your research questions are still appropriate and do not require revision. Why do you want to separate undergraduates?"

Chris: "Our research indicates that in the first year (in particular) or first two years (in general), undergraduates face the greatest risk, so we would like to talk to them. But we also want to talk to seasoned undergraduates who have been successful for at least two years."

FG Expert: "Sounds good, Chris. Do you want to separate those who have financial aid from those who do not? Do you think they will have different perspectives? Similarly, do you want to separate those who are working on campus from those who are working off campus?"

Chris: "Hmm . . . more interesting questions. So, are you suggesting that we separate those who receive financial aid from those who do not but who may be working? And, perhaps those who are working on campus from those who are working off campus?"

FG Expert: "No, I'm not suggesting anything; I'm just asking if that is important to the research. Remember, focus groups are typically conducted among homogeneous groups of participants. As we continue to think through that, let's look through your draft Moderator's Guide. As I mentioned at our last meeting, I think your topic questions look good. The questions you need to ask yourselves are: How do they apply to each of the proposed groups? And to what extent do they answer the research question? First, let's review your warm-up and wrap-up questions."

Chris: "I know you differentiate between warm-up questions and ice-breakers, but I am not sure we completely understand the difference. As you can see our first thought was to ask everyone to tell us something interesting about themselves that even their friends might not know about them."

FG Expert: "That is an icebreaker designed to get everyone participating in the conversation, but it is not in any way related to the topic of the focus group. It's better to ask them a question that also engages them in the topic. For example, 'As you were preparing to come to college for your first year, what most excited you about attending college and what was your greatest concern?'"

Chris: "Ah, yes, they all get an opportunity to introduce themselves and we get an idea about how great a concern cost was. Let's use those."

Expert: "Yes, we accomplish both. And if we have students write their answers to those questions on five-inch-by-eight-inch cards, we have some written data to analyze. Okay, good start. What about a good wrap-up question?"

The conversation continues as the group edits the topic questions together and simultaneously considers the extent to which they can be meaningfully answered by each of the proposed populations. They agree to include first- and second-year undergraduates who are working on campus, first- and second-year undergraduates who are working off campus, third- and fourth-year undergraduates who are working on campus, and third- and fourth-year undergraduates who are working off campus. The FG Expert raises a concern about how we would know if they are working off campus, and the committee agrees to contact the Institutional Research (IR) office to inquire about that. The FG Expert explains to the committee that if IR cannot identify who works off campus, they could include one or more screening questions in their invitation and RSVP asking participants to self-identify. The committee decides not to separate those who are receiving financial aid from those who are not. And, as requested by the FG Expert, they agree to develop another complete draft of their Moderator's Guide for the next meeting. (Appendix K contains the Moderator's Guide.)

6

STEP #4: SELECT AND TRAIN THE MODERATORS

The Research Tool

Moderators are the primary research tool in focus group methodology since they both collect the data and provide the initial analysis. Moderators must be good listeners and empathic and flexible facilitators, and they must be trained to conduct focus groups. This chapter explains the role of moderators, the characteristics required of them, and how to identify and train them.

Because moderators are a critical component of the focus group, careful consideration of individual styles and skills must be made before inviting someone to be a moderator. In short, moderating a focus group takes a variety of skills. Mentors need to not only listen well, connect and summarize concepts, be flexible, and be patient but also keep track of time, cover all of the topics, and take notes, all while communicating warmth and creating a friendly, open atmosphere.

Shirley and her team, in consultation with the FG Expert, have drafted Moderator's Guides for each population and made any required modifications in the research questions. While they continue to edit their Moderator's Guides, Shirley returns to the FG Expert to discuss who will moderate all of these groups. She and a few members of her team want to volunteer to moderate some of the groups, and some have experience in focus group moderation. But no client should moderate any of his or her own focus groups because of potential bias. Moderators collect and analyze the data and so moderating a group discussing one's own project presents a situation that is simply too tantalizing. Both intentional and unconscious bias will likely creep in and corrupt the data and results.

The FG Expert will discuss the style and skill required in moderators and explain that we typically use co-moderators and offer them some reward for their efforts because this work usually exceeds their job descriptions. Remember that *moderators* refers to all those who moderate a group, and *co-moderators* refers to the two moderators who work together on a particular focus group. While Shirley understands the potential bias in conducting the focus groups themselves, she questions if co-moderators are really necessary, especially since that will increase the budget. Fortunately, the FG Expert has a pool of trained FG moderators from which to draw. The FG Expert also offers to train Shirley and the members of her team and add them to the list of trained moderators for future focus groups.

> Shirley: "Our Moderator's Guides are proceeding nicely, and we think we have some good questions to ask. Several members of my committee volunteered to lead the focus groups, which sounds great to me. What do you think?"

> FG Expert: "As a general rule, Shirley, we do not lead our own focus groups because we are too close to the project to be objective about it. We do not want a moderator to overreact to a statement a participant makes. We also want the participants to feel free to speak comfortably without concern about who will be listening to them as they share their thoughts and feelings. We also do not want to risk having moderators lead the conversation in a direction they think it should go."

> Shirley: "I am sure that all of our committee members would meet those qualifications."

> FG Expert: "I am sure they would, Shirley; however, we do not know whether any will be perceived as biased in some way by some of the participants."

> Shirley: "Okay, good point. I am learning a lot about conducting focus groups. So, who should we ask to moderate the focus groups?"

> FG Expert: "We have a list of people whom we have trained and who have moderated previous focus groups for us. We want to train you and your committee as part of the process and add you to the list so you can moderate future focus groups for us. Also, we typically use two moderators in each group, and we reward them for their work."

> Shirley: "We would love to participate in the training. Sounds like a lot more money to double the number of moderators. Is this all really necessary?"

FG Expert: "We have found that co-moderators significantly enhance both the actual focus group discussion and the data analyses. Co-moderators often hear things differently, so they can discuss those differences as part of the data analyses, which results in more accurate data. We also try to introduce some diversity into the focus groups by pairing men and women or moderators of different races or ethnicities. We like to enhance the chances that each participant might find someone they can relate to."

Shirley: "All good points but I thought we would be doing the data analyses."

FG Expert: "We developed this method for conducting focus groups in higher education because we know that we have a lot of smart faculty and administrators who have both training and experience in conducting discussions and research and data analyses. With a little training, most of us can do a good job moderating the groups as well as analyzing the data."

Shirley: "Okay, so more specifically, what kinds of folks are we looking for?"

Moderator Role

The moderator gathers information from group participants that addresses the purpose of the focus group by inviting participants to share their attitudes and opinions (Greenbaum, 1998). The moderator establishes a rapport within the group by initiating a conversation around a topic, asking questions that delve deeper into participants' responses, and encouraging open participation that may include both positive and negative comments. (More details about how to elicit information from participants will be covered later in this chapter.) Since the main role of moderators is to gather information from participants, they should talk very little during the group and must be comfortable with silence. Typically, when there is silence people want to fill it; therefore, silence can be a powerful tool for prompting discussion. To ensure the moderator is listening carefully and getting relevant and accurate information from participants, the moderator should summarize the discussion frequently.

The moderator should make efforts to ensure that everyone in the group is participating. The moderator should encourage participants to agree and disagree among themselves and challenge each other. When a participant states an opinion the moderator should ask the other participants their thoughts about the person's statement, thus creating a dialogue among the participants.

The most important piece of the moderator's role is to gather information that will address the purpose set by the researchers for the focus group project. To do this the moderator must cover all of the topics adequately and allow enough time for each topic so the participants can thoroughly express their thoughts and opinions. Sometimes when participants share their thoughts and opinions, side topics can manifest. Side topics are topics that relate to the main focus group topic but were not explicitly asked. For instance, in a focus group session about discovering vision and direction for the institution, the moderator asks a question regarding the three most important areas on which a leader should focus his or her efforts within the first three months. The participants give a listing of ideas and areas that need to be addressed, such as identity or brand and specific policies, but at some point in the conversation a participant brings up how leadership in other units impacts the participant's unit and not only complicates once-simple matters but also makes decisions that directly impact that unit's business. At this point, the moderator has to choose whether or not to explore this topic further. Although not directly related to the main purpose of the focus group project, the participant has brought up an issue that leadership may need to know about or address. The moderator should cautiously explore this topic, asking probing questions of the participants and getting others to share their thoughts; however, the conversation here cannot be allowed to go on for too long, as it takes away from the other topic areas that need to be covered. The moderator must carefully balance the time allotted to this new topic while gathering enough meaningful information.

Throughout the group session, the moderator should remain neutral and objective and not offer an opinion or thoughts about a topic. Sometimes participants will ask the moderator about a definition, common practice, or procedure. The moderator should not respond to the participants and should instead say they can answer the questions at the end of the session or ask participants to address the question. Additionally, participants may incorrectly state something about data or processes. Again, the moderator should remain detached and not correct participants during the session.

Moderator Characteristics

First and foremost, moderators should be able to *express themselves clearly*. The group topics and questions should be conveyed plainly and distinctly so that participants understand what is being asked. Moderators should be *quick learners* with the ability to comprehend new concepts immediately, and to think fast and assemble ideas from multiple perspectives or points in time. During the focus group participants may make comments or statements at different points in the conversation that require the moderators to make connections between concepts. Being able to make quick connections during a group is related to another important characteristic—being a *good listener*. Moderators should speak less than one-third of the time, thereby dedicating most of their time to listening. They need to be able to not only hear participants' statements but also assess tone. A participant may make a joking or sarcastic comment during the group, and it is up to the moderators to discern the difference.

Flexibility is another key skill the moderators should possess. The Moderator's Guide serves as the guidebook for the moderators. The structure implies a linear approach to facilitating a group. However, participants are not privy to the plan and may give answers to questions that appear later in the guide. They may also deviate from a question and offer information on a related topic. Moderators must be able to perceive when this is happening and understand how to refocus participants without disrupting the conversation flow or friendly environment. Furthermore, moderators have to be alert when a topic was covered earlier in the conversation and not allow the discussion to be repeated. Flexibility in the face of the unanticipated is an essential skill when identifying moderators for focus groups.

Moderators should care about the participants and the group dynamics and be able to demonstrate *empathy*. Participants will not be open and honest with a moderator they perceive as egocentric or unable to understand their point of view. The moderator must carefully balance opinions and comments from all of the participants and cannot focus on one or two individuals.

Lastly, moderators should be *knowledgeable* but not all-knowing. Their main role is to facilitate the discussion; therefore, they need to know something about the topic so that they understand the discussion, but they should not assert their opinions or beliefs during the discussion. They should also not be directly involved with the project or have a self-interest in the project outcomes so as to minimize their influence during the group session and data analyses.

Co-Moderators

Once the pool of moderators has been identified, the moderators should be paired for each focus group session—two people should facilitate the conversation and gather data that achieves the project purpose. Because people will hear and note different things, the use of co-moderators helps ensure that accurate and representative data are collected from the group. One major consideration in selecting co-moderators is the demographic makeup of the group participants. It is helpful if the participants see themselves in some way in at least one of the moderators. If the focus group is with undergraduate students, then it may be useful to pair a senior or graduate student with a seasoned moderator. When conducting a focus group with senior-level administrators, the moderators should be professionals who understand senior-leadership's role and have a higher level degree and skill sets. Demographic characteristics, including age, employment level, gender, ethnicity, and race, should be considered when selecting co-moderators.

Moderator Duties

The moderators have specific duties that they need to undertake during the focus group project. Moderators must attend a one- to two-hour training session. This session will give the moderators an overview of the project, methods for handling various situations that may arise during the sessions, and an opportunity to review the Moderator's Guide and clarify any confusing topics or questions. Following the training and before the group session is conducted, moderators should meet with their co-moderator to discuss logistics of the session such as time of arrival, question and topic assignments, agreements on who handles late arrivers or disruptive participants, and contact information including cell phone numbers. Note that because the person who starts the group is seen as the leader, the moderator who most closely represents the participants should begin the conversation. The moderators should allow for two hours to conduct the focus group session. After the session, co-moderators should allow for two to three hours per group to review the recording, compile notes, and summarize themes they heard. Once individual summaries are completed, co-moderators should meet to compare notes and produce a final summary report that includes their combined report along with both individual reports. The time dedicated to this part should be no more than two hours. Lastly, the moderators should attend a 1- to 2-hour debriefing session with the FG Expert to discuss themes. In total, the moderators will commit 9 to 12 hours for the first group and an additional 5 hours for each subsequent group they moderate for the project.

Moderator Training

In a few days Shirley returns with a list of potential moderators that she would like to review with the FG Expert. Now she wants to know what the training will entail.

> Shirley: "I assume that you will train the moderators along with some of our committee members."

FG Expert: "Yes, we have a training guide that I will e-mail to you. We typically train the new moderators and offer a refresher to the moderators who have worked with us before. Then we brief the moderators on the current project and review the Moderator's Guide with them and ask for their feedback."

Shirley: "Why are we asking the moderators for feedback on the Moderator's Guide?"

FG Expert: "The moderators offer a fresh perspective on the guide, especially those who have conducted focus groups before. They often catch something we missed and are very good at pointing out how questions might be reworded to be clearer to participants. We want to make sure that our questions are clear and are asked in the same manner by all moderators to ensure that we get good conversations and good data."

A training session should be held for all moderators about two weeks before the first group is scheduled. The training session provides information about the focus group project's purpose and context, and the tools and methods needed to conduct the group session. The training outlines the skills moderators need to rely on during the session, gives examples of what to do in various situations, and presents solutions to common problems. Also during the session, moderators should review and make suggestions to the Moderator's Guide, and discuss and clarify topics, questions, and prompts. Since the client and stakeholders asked for the focus groups to be conducted, they have the big picture and will tell the FG Expert whether or not the important content is covered. The moderators, in contrast, are focused on conducting the focus groups and have a sense of the extent to which these topic questions will be understood by the participants. If the moderators do not understand the topic or questions, then it is likely that the participants will not either and the moderators will not be able to explain it to them. The moderators offer "fresh eyes" on something that others have been reviewing and editing for weeks. Finally, moderators meet their co-moderators.

Although training sessions can be time-consuming for all, the time expended improves the project and cements the moderators as a group that each member can rely on as the process unfolds. The training session should include the following skills and issues.

Nonverbal Behavior

Nonverbal behaviors include facial expressions; eye movement and gaze; body language and posture; personal appearance; gestures; playing with objects; and voice tone, loudness, and speed, among others. These behaviors act as signals or clues and communicate thoughts and feelings. Paying attention to and using nonverbals can be one of the most effective tools when conducting a focus group.

The moderator must pay attention to his or her own use of nonverbals. He or she must look engaged in the conversation by sitting upright and leaning in a little bit. This action signals to the participants that the moderator is *a good listener*, a vital characteristic for moderators. People know when someone is listening and paying attention to them and respond to that by giving more or less information, so it is imperative that the moderator makes certain that participants feel that what he or she is saying is important and useful.

While paying attention to their posture, moderators should also note if they are nodding their heads in agreement or disagreement when participants are speaking. A sign of a good listener, or someone who is *empathic* (another characteristic of a good moderator), is someone who is actively engaged in the other person's side of the conversation and reveals this active engagement in head nods or some type of facial expression. But, moderators must remain neutral and unbiased; therefore, they should not lead participants by nodding while someone is speaking. Head nods can be seen as affirmations; during the group affirmations can lead to participants saying things they think the moderator wants to hear—providing the "correct answer." For instance, a moderator asks about sense of belonging to a group of students. Most of the participants discuss a positive sense of belonging, while one mentions that it is difficult. The moderator nods to demonstrate empathy toward the participant and to give that person a safe space to talk; however, this head nodding causes participants to think that the moderator only wants to hear negative thoughts or struggles. With a simple nodding of the head, the moderator has inadvertently shifted the participants' perceptions of the group and their role within the group.

Balancing Input

Sometimes a group will include participants who speak only to the moderator; are very reserved; or, conversely, are quite outspoken. While it can be difficult, there are several methods to balance input so that the former speak more and the latter speak less. First, the moderator should subtly look away from the participant speaking. This behavior signifies that the responding participant should be addressing the group, not the moderator. This helps create a discussion and not an interview setting. Second, the moderator can look around the table to see the nonverbal behaviors being used by others, which can be leveraged by the moderator to include others in the conversation by simply saying, "I see others are nodding their heads, what does that mean?" or "Others are nodding, does that mean you agree with this statement?" This is a particularly effective way of bringing in reserved or quiet participants. Third, looking away from a particularly loquacious person can signify that he or she is dominating the conversation and should give others a chance to participate.

Handling Silence

Being comfortable with silence emerges as critically important. It can also be a difficult skill to develop, as many people find silence deeply awkward and unnerving. There will be many times during the group when there is a break in the discussion or the moderator asks a question and no one responds, thus creating silence. The moderator should not be the first person to fill that silence. A useful tip is for the moderator to slowly count to 10 after asking a question. This gives the moderator time to let the silence settle, look around the room for nonverbal behaviors, and allow participants to think about their responses. Most of the time the participants feel the need to fill the silence after a few seconds. If this does not happen, then the moderator may refer to the follow-up prompts included in the Moderator's Guide. The follow-up prompt can be a restatement of the question or a neutral prompt that is not specific to the topic but encourages people to talk. Prompts can ask participants to explain further, give an example, ask others what they think, or ask if others had similar experiences or thoughts. These prompts can be used to facilitate conversation or drive people to think more deeply about the question.

Common Problems

Problems can sometimes occur during the focus group session. These problems can range from simple—"dead" topic—to extreme—"upset" participant. Moderators can also play a role in problems that occur. It is important to think about these issues when selecting moderators to minimize the impact and occurrence of potential problems. Training can help moderators learn how to avoid and address these common problems.

Although a lot of work has been done in the beginning to make sure the focus group topic can sustain a 60- to 90-minute conversation and the questions are open ended, there are times when the questions or topics are confusing or boring to the group and the moderator cannot stimulate a conversation. When this occurs moderators can reframe questions or use probing questions to stimulate deeper thought. Ultimately, if the participants cannot answer the questions, the moderators have to move on to the next topic.

Upset participants can disrupt the group by using offensive language or aggressive behavior. Other times a group topic could trigger an emotional response from participants that places them in crisis. Co-moderators have to determine prior to the group who will speak to or remove a participant who is being disruptive or having a personal crisis.

Moderators who are too rigid during the group can impact the flow of conversation and open atmosphere. Although the topics and questions of focus groups are presented in a linear pattern, there are times when a question is asked and participants' responses relate to topic areas that are listed later in the Moderator's Guide. Furthermore, the topics do not have set "talk times"—a time limit is not given to each topic, and it is up to the moderators to determine when to move to the next set of questions or topic. Moderators have to remain flexible with the guide and refrain from stopping the conversation because of time or order. Conversely, when moderators are too flexible they may not cover all of the topics. It is important for the moderators to understand when they need to allow participants to have an energetic conversation, while making sure all of the topics are covered.

It is important that moderators be knowledgeable about the topic so they can ask probing or follow-up questions as needed. But problems can arise in a group when the moderator uses his or her knowledge to correct a participant, thus effectively negating the idea that there are no right or wrong answers and all opinions should be shared. If participants incorrectly state a fact, the moderators should not correct them. Focus groups are intended to learn about perceptions or opinions to make improvements elsewhere; therefore, moderators can ask others what they think about a statement or an opinion to understand if everyone shares a similar belief. At the end of the group the moderator can talk with the participant and give the correct information if necessary.

Whether the focus group has a dead topic, a participant in crisis, or a charismatic participant who always answers the questions, moderators can fall into the trap of focusing too much on one participant. They can use this person as a "crutch" when there is silence, knowing the person will answer the questions, or they can turn the session into a counseling session using verbal and nonverbal behaviors as affirmations. Moderators must pay attention to their behavior during the group. Saying things like "that's good" or "excellent" or head nodding can lead participants to think the moderators want specific or "correct" answers. It can also lead to turning the group into a counseling session where participants share their hopes and fears and not their opinions and beliefs about the topic.

How to Handle Challenging Participants

Perhaps the greatest fear or concern among moderators is what happens when they encounter challenges or problems with one or more of the participants. How do they get shy participants to talk or talkative participants to talk less? What do they do if someone dominates the conversation or is always the first one to answer a question? What do they say to a participant who identifies himself or herself (legitimately or not) as an expert on this topic? How do they keep all participants engaged in the conversation? And, perhaps the greatest fear is what if one participant becomes disruptive to the group in some way, perhaps because the person is trying to control the discussion or perhaps because the topic has affected him or her in a very personal, emotional way? Krueger (1998) and Krueger and Casey (2015) identified several types of challenging participants:

- experts and influentials
- dominant talkers
- ramblers and wanderers
- quiet and shy participants
- inattentive participants
- disruptive participants (p. 58)

Working with people who are experts or regard themselves as an *expert or influential* person is challenging when they consciously or unconsciously attempt to control the group. This is one of the reasons we create homogeneous focus groups—so that everyone has knowledge about the topic and no one is an expert. People with expertise and influence might also be *dominant talkers*. Other dominant talkers may merely be prone to talking a lot but not saying much. Participants who are extroverts tend to think through problems by discussing them with others, but this can be distracting, particularly to those participants who are introverts who typically process their thoughts internally and only share them when they are more fully formed. Whether participants are *experts and influentials* or *dominant talkers*, moderators can diplomatically remind them, and the other participants, that each individual was invited to the group because he or she has experience with, and knowledge about, this particular topic. Skilled moderators also remind them that we want to hear from all of the participants. They might say, "You seem very knowledgeable about this topic and we appreciate your input. We know that all of the participants have knowledge and experience with the topic and we want to hear what everyone thinks."

Extroverted participants may also be seen as *ramblers and wanderers* as they are processing their thoughts. Other participants may just naturally ramble or wander through conversations without clearly thinking about their ideas or putting together a coherent statement of ideas; and they are often unaware of the impact this has on the other participants. Both introverts and extroverts can be *quiet and shy* in unfamiliar situations with a group of strangers. The primary goal of writing good, engaging warm-up questions is to get everyone talking as soon as possible in the group so that even the shy and quiet participants will feel comfortable participating. Beyond the warm-up, quiet and shy participants may still need some encouragement to participate in the topic discussions. Skilled moderators are aware of nonverbal signs that the quiet or shy person is actually very engaged but perhaps not yet finished processing and ready to participate. Others will be intimidated by those who speak constantly and may be perceived as experts. While introverted participants need to be encouraged to talk more, extroverted participants need to be reminded to gather and organize their thoughts before sharing so we have sufficient time to hear from all the participants. Skilled moderators will call on quiet and shy participants as they simultaneously try to quiet the participants who are talking too much—"Let's hear from some other participants; how about you, [participant's name]?"

Skilled moderators are able to read the nonverbal signs of the nonparticipants to determine if they are quiet and shy but engaged, or whether they are *inattentive participants*. Inattentive participants should more quickly be brought back into the conversation before they tune out completely. The skilled moderator must be aware, however, if there is a reason for these individuals being inattentive: perhaps some life situation or they are having a bad day, or perhaps they do not actually know much about the topic, in which case they might be left alone after one or two attempts to engage them. Perhaps the most challenging participants are the *disruptive participants*, whether they are being deliberately disruptive or have become the focus of the group because they have experienced a very emotional response to the topic. The latter is most likely to happen in groups dealing with sensitive topics. Either way, the disruptive participant must be diplomatically brought into a more appropriate role in the group or in extreme situations be asked to leave the group so that others can have a productive discussion. Skilled moderators remember that this is not a counseling group but a qualitative research project attempting to gather data to help a larger group of people. That said, they will also ensure that the emotionally distraught participant is not allowed to leave without some discussion and offers of help outside the group. If the disruption threatens the accuracy of the focus group such that we would have to conduct another focus group, the skilled moderator might say, "Let's take a five-minute break to visit the restroom and get some more food or just stretch and reflect and refocus. We will return to this group and sit in different seats." Sometimes the break will be sufficient, and sometimes the moderator will use the break to escort the disruptive person from the room, making sure to graciously thank the person for his or her participation and valued contributions.

Krueger (1998) and Krueger and Casey (2015) also discussed a variety of methods for dealing with challenging participants. Skilled moderators are aware of, and thus come prepared for, these potential challenges and are attentive to the behavior of the participants from the moment they enter the room. They anticipate potential problems and are prepared to deal with them. They are constantly monitoring the expressions and tone of voice of all the participants, not just the one who is speaking.

The best way to deal with participant problems is to prevent them to the extent possible. This is one of the reasons we are so meticulous with the planning of the focus groups. We carefully identify the populations and segments who are knowledgeable about the topic. We also carefully build and edit the Moderator's Guide so it is easily understood and flows smoothly. In addition, we are aware of what may be sensitive topics. Finally, we carefully choose and train moderators who are skilled at leading group discussions and completing data analyses. Faculty and administrative staff may have an advantage in dealing with these situations, because they have a lot of experience working with similar situations among their students and colleagues. One of the advantages of using faculty and staff as moderators is that they are familiar with the culture of the institution and the populations in the institutional community.

Skilled moderators use good reflective statements to summarize the content related to a particular topic to make sure they understand the content of the discussion, to determine whether there is any new content to be offered, and to move to the next topic. They also use good reflective statements to redirect the conversation. Flattery is often very effective and diplomacy is essential. The following are some phrases that might be used to reflect a feeling or attitude back to the speaker:

- "You seem to have some special expertise related to this topic but [and] . . ."
- "You seem to be passionate [or angry or hurt or depressed] about this topic but [and] . . ."
- "Thank you; that is helpful. . . ."

The following are some phrases that can be used to encourage discussion and distract attention from someone who is dominating:

- "What do others think about this topic?"
- "Do others agree or disagree with these thoughts?"
- "We would like to hear from others; what do you think, [participant's name]?"

These are some phrases that can be used to redirect the conversation from someone who is dominating:

- "This is a good discussion about which there are several different opinions. I would like to remind everyone that a fundamental guideline for focus groups is that we want to be sure to listen politely to all points of view. It is okay to disagree and there is no need to reach consensus."
- "You have been very generous with your comments. We would like to hear the thoughts of the rest of the participants."

While it is impossible to memorize a specific response to each potential situation, the preceding ideas and phrases should help moderators to build a repertoire of potential responses that they are comfortable using. Each comment they make should fit both the situation and their personality so that it is genuine. Skilled moderators know that their job is to gather data using the Moderator's Guide and their own skills. No one likes to hurt a participant's feelings, but the ultimate goal is to gather data that will be used to improve the situation for the population these participants represent, not just these participants.

The Moderator's Training Guide is provided in Appendix L.

James Vignette (Access)

Recall that in their last conversation the FG Expert offered James and his teammates the list from which to identify potential moderators for their focus groups. They could also suggest others who may not be on the list but the committee thinks would be good moderators. The FG Expert also asked them to consider some other questions about who should be chosen as moderators for groups of underrepresented students. How appropriate is it for faculty and staff, many of whom are older and from majority groups, to conduct these focus groups? Would it be better to train graduate students from underrepresented groups to moderate the focus groups? Typically, the FG Expert suggests that focus group participants feel more comfortable talking with moderators who have some common characteristic such as age, race, ethnicity, or gender. Finally, how or will the moderators be compensated? Once the type of moderators who are appropriate for the project are identified, the FG Expert will offer to help James choose specific moderators. The FG Expert will offer to train the moderators plus James and his committee to build the community of trained focus group moderators for future projects.

FG Expert: "James, what have you and your committee decided about who you want to co-moderate your focus groups?"

James: "First of all, we agreed that we should choose at least one co-moderator for each focus group who is from an underrepresented group. We also want co-moderators who are of different races and genders to the extent possible. We also think graduate assistants [GAs] might be most age appropriate to act as co-moderators. However, we did not find many GAs on your list and do not know of many ourselves."

FG Expert: "As you might guess, the list of GA moderators turns over frequently because they graduate and leave the institution. So, we often have to identify some current GAs. Let's contact the dean of graduate studies and the associate deans in the colleges as well as department chairs to see if they can give us some recommendations. We can then interview and select a few good candidates. Some students in helping disciplines consider this to be valuable professional experience."

James: "Sounds good. So, what is the training process and how long does it last?"

FG Expert: "The training involves two parts. First, we train moderators about the focus group process, the role of co-moderators, and characteristics of good co-moderators. It is somewhat informal and we have a handout for them. Second, we walk through the Moderator's Guide with them and ask them to assess how accurate and easy to understand the questions are. Will the focus group participants be able to understand what the questions are asking and interpret them in the same way as they were intended? That is, do they understand what each question is asking and do they have suggestions? Have we missed any questions or are some redundant? We always find that we can improve the Moderator's Guide after this session."

James: "Great; let's get started. I will set up the training and make copies of the handouts. . . ."

The conversation continues as James and the FG Expert compare calendars and the FG Expert asks James to work on the logistics for the focus groups before the next meeting. There is a copy of the Moderator's Training Guide in Appendix L.

Chris Vignette (Affordability)

Recall that the FG Expert asked the committee to find out whether or not IR or perhaps the financial aid office could determine which undergraduate students work on and off campus to determine whether or not they could include them in separate focus groups in this project on the impact of college costs on student success. The committee also agreed to create another draft of their Moderator's Guide. Now they are ready to discuss how to select and train the moderators.

> Chris: "We researched the question about what data we may have that can help us determine which students work off campus. There does not seem to be any data that will reliably do that for us. We can, however, identify students who work on campus using our student information system. What do you recommend?"

> FG Expert: "We can develop one or two screening questions to include as part of the invitations. For example, do you work on campus, off campus, both, or neither? We can use those data to place participants into groups. And we may want to include a couple of groups of students who do not work for comparison."

> Chris: "Interesting thoughts as always. Let's do that, that is, ask the screening questions and add two groups of undergraduates who do not work. This may require revisiting our sampling plan as well as our Moderator's Guide and perhaps our research question. We can do that as a group before our next meeting. So, we are ready to discuss selecting the moderators. Some of our committee members were hoping we could lead the focus groups, but we understand that you have told all previous committees that they should not lead their own groups."

> FG Expert: "Remember to include in your plan four additional groups—two of first- and second-year undergraduates who do not work and two of third- and fourth-year undergraduates who do not work. Right? And, regarding moderators you are correct, Chris, we do not lead our own groups as we may be biased in asking the questions or listening to the participants' responses. We will train you for future focus group projects,

however. Some of us are also long past our student days, so the participants may not respond as well to us as they might respond to graduate assistants or perhaps some senior students who are majoring in the social sciences and preparing to graduate."

Chris: "Using graduate students certainly makes sense, but I am not sure about undergraduates. Are they too close to the population, perhaps members of the population?"

FG Expert: "Let's see if we can find some good graduate students, although they may have as recently as last year been members of one of the populations as well. However, I think they are a good choice and we can look for graduate students who completed their undergraduate degrees at another institution. We also like to use co-moderators to conduct our focus groups and preferably co-moderators of different racial and ethnic backgrounds or genders."

Chris: "We appreciate your focus on diversity. I understand you have a list of some potential moderators. Perhaps we can come up with a few names ourselves. What will the training consist of?"

The FG Expert discusses the primary components of training: training in focus group methods and briefing the moderators on the topic as well as reviewing the draft Moderator's Guide. The FG Expert also tasks Chris and the committee to double- and triple-check all of the logistics before the next meeting.

7

STEP #5: CONDUCT THE FOCUS GROUPS

It's All About Logistics

Logistics matters when conducting focus groups. While a popular mantra and book series counsels us, "Don't sweat the small stuff," we advise obsessing about the details in preparing to conduct focus groups. Participants provide the data for analysis, and the best data arise from conversations that participants find engaging, indeed absorbing, and that keep their attention. Frustrations and distractions intrude on the experience, become the center of thought and conversation, and may usurp the group's purpose. Locations that are hard to find, rooms that are too hot or too cold, chairs that are uncomfortable, food that arrives late or is inedible, supplies that are missing, or technology that fails will distract the participants and moderators. A single large or multiple small distractions may affect the quality of conversations and therefore the quality of the data. Thus, "sweating the small stuff" is critical to focus group success. This chapter discusses the myriad details to be considered in establishing optimal conditions for focus groups because logistics is crucial. Each item discussed matters because its successful fulfillment or implementation helps keep the participants (and moderators) attentive to the discussion, the entire reason for their presence. A checklist in Appendix O presents the items in a project management format.

It is now time to conduct the focus groups! In addition to continuously fine-tuning their Research Proposal, identifying participants, editing and re-editing the Moderator's Guide, and selecting and training the moderators, Shirley and her team have been working on logistics. Most of these details are included in the Research Proposal, but wanting to make certain everything is right, Shirley returns to review all of the final logistical details with the FG Expert.

FG Expert: "Hi, Shirley. I see that we are approaching the dates of our focus groups, and I wanted to call or meet to review all of the logistical details for the groups."

Shirley: "Good timing; I was just reviewing my list."

FG Expert: "So, here are some of the things on my mind. How are the RSVPs going? How many groups are filled? Are we prepared to send out reminder e-mails or text messages the day before?"

Shirley: "That is the main point that is bothering me. For a couple of the student groups we only have three or four RSVPs. As I recall you said the minimum number is about seven or eight."

FG Expert: "Correct Shirley, 7 to 10 is the ideal group size, especially if any of our student participants are quiet and not inclined to participate much. I am uncomfortable having 2 co-moderators lead a discussion with 3 or 4 students."

Shirley: "I agree. So what should we do? Cancel a couple of groups?"

FG Expert: "If we cancel groups we will likely not have the two or three groups needed to represent each segment. We asked students to indicate all of the proposed times for which they were available. Can any of them be moved into another group? Can we call some of them to see about changing to another group?"

Shirley: "We can try that. What if it doesn't work?"

FG Expert: "We cross our fingers and hope for the best. Too often students do not RSVP but show up anyway. If we only get three to four or five, we can conduct the group with one moderator so as not to overwhelm the students. However, we must be careful to note this in the analyses. If they are largely in agreement with the other focus groups, we can feel a little more comfortable."

Shirley: "Okay, I will work on this. What else is on your list?"

FG Expert: "Just a few other thoughts about logistics . . ."

Logistical Decisions Prior to Issuing Invitations

This chapter refers to the Organizer, who is the person in charge of logistics, arrives in advance of the focus group with the supplies, and confirms that all is well. The Organizer may be a single person or the responsibilities may be shared among several people; the Organizer may be the client, the FG Expert, a moderator, or someone whose only responsibility is logistics. The Organizer makes certain that the room is properly set up and ready for the participants and that catering (if used) has arrived and has set up the food and drinks. The Organizer also makes certain that the moderators arrive and are ready to conduct the group.

A series of decisions must be made before issuing a single invitation to participate in a focus group. These include choosing the dates and times of day as well as the space in which the group will meet, and deciding about refreshments, gifts, and incentives. All of this information will be included on the invitation in order to inform and encourage participation.

Timing

Determining when the group will be conducted is somewhat dependent on population and segment, so keen knowledge of these is key. Time and day can affect faculty, administrators, staff, and students differently, thereby impacting participation. It might be easier to get faculty, administrators, and staff to attend a breakfast or lunch group, particularly if a meal is served, while students might more readily attend an evening group. Some days of the week might work better for a particular population. Time and day matter as some populations may be affected by semester schedules. Particularly busy times of the semester (e.g., the first two weeks, midterms, finals) impede participation for some segments (e.g., students and faculty) while spring break may facilitate it for others (e.g., advisers). While it is difficult to accommodate everyone, it is important to consider factors that may negatively impact participation levels for each segment of the population. Simply put, finding a convenient meeting time or event to conduct focus groups yields greater participation. There might be a luncheon that can be used as a setting for a focus group, a time during a conference when participants can gather, or a regularly scheduled meeting that can be turned into a focus group. Thinking creatively about meeting spaces, locations, and times can have a positive effect on participation rates.

Since multiple groups will be conducted for each segment, decisions should be made about whether or not all groups should be conducted at the same day, time, and location. There are advantages and disadvantages to each decision. Conducting all groups at the same time reduces scheduling logistics and means that all data are collected in one day. If some participants do not show up, resulting in a very small group, the group can be integrated into another focus group, if appropriate. Standardizing the time and location, however, may exclude population segments who cannot or are unlikely to attend at that particular time. The FG Expert must weigh data collection and logistic convenience against accessibility for the participants.

Facilities

Locations must be convenient to the participants, easy to find, and in a neutral location. Universities often occupy large areas and contain lots of buildings, many of which do not have actual physical addresses, streets in front of them, or adequate nearby parking. While it is likely that nearly everyone on campus knows where many buildings are, some participants may not know where a particular building resides, so invitations should give clear directions that identify the building, its address, and nearby buildings. When participants are community members who may be unfamiliar with the campus, provide maps that include driving, parking, and walking directions and maybe even escorts to the building and perhaps the room. Make certain that parking is as easy as possible and provide parking passes or advise participants that you will take care of any parking tickets. Choose a building that is not affiliated with the topic. If the focus group's purpose is to discuss the upper administration, for example, schedule a location away from the administration building so that participants do not accidentally run into involved administrators right before or after the group.

The rooms should also be convenient and easy to find once in the building; prepare and put up directional signs. The space should be relatively quiet and somewhat private, rather than in an area with a lot of activity. Avoid any place with glass walls where participants can be easily seen or distracted. Visit the room before finalizing it to make certain that recent renovations have not rendered it unusable for your purposes. The room should be large enough to accommodate a conference table, 9 to 12 comfortable chairs, and a table for food or snacks and drinks. If possible, avoid rooms that are overly large, as the group will feel swamped by the space. If the room or conference table is significantly larger than needed, ascertain that you will be able to cluster the needed chairs at one end and perhaps remove the rest or at least push them away. Make certain that the room is not a pass-through to some other space that may be used. Consider noise and avoid rooms with nearby construction or loud foot traffic. Note where the restrooms are located. If conducting several groups at once in a single area, make sure there is space to set up a table outside of the main entrance to check in participants on arrival.

Incentives and Gifts

Incentives increase participation rates. They impress upon participants that we value their time and commitment. Announce the incentive in the invitation, such as a drawing for a door prize, with the "must be present to win" proviso, as this helps ensure that participants actually show up to the group. These can either be for each group or, especially if running a large number of groups, collect all attendees' names and hold a drawing for a high-value item at the end of all groups. In this case, be certain to let everyone know who won.

Thank you gifts for each participant show appreciation for their time and build goodwill. Gifts and incentives need not be elaborate or expensive but should be appropriate for the population. They can range from institution swag such as key chains, USB flash drives, drink bottles, coffee mugs, pens, or notepads to movie tickets or a voucher for coffee or a free meal. Higher value incentives might be gift cards, clothing, or electronics. Larger or more expensive incentives can also be added via a lottery with one drawing per group or one drawing across groups in a segment, and so forth. We can also offer a "small token of our appreciation" gift to each participant plus a chance to win a larger prize. If every participant receives a "prize," these gifts can range from $1 to $10. If there will only be one or two random winners, larger grand prizes can start at $50 or more.

Refreshments

Refreshments should be provided to every group in addition to and not in place of incentives. Refreshments should be appropriate to time of day and population. Refreshments can range from full meals (breakfast, lunch, or dinner) to snack options (bagels, granola bars, cookies). Offer meals if the group is conducted during mealtimes; indeed, this might enhance the likelihood of participation, as everyone is busy and needs to eat. Scheduling a focus group of administrators early in the morning or around noon and providing them breakfast or lunch encourages participation, as they will not lose much more of their workday than normal.

Pizza, cookies, and soda can be enticing for students, but not for faculty, administrators, or staff. Noise, smell, and interruptions caused by the refreshments should be considered. Avoid situations where there may be a clanging of dishes during the group or where people need to continually get up from the table to retrieve food. If offering a meal, select either a self-serving buffet or boxed meals and choose foods that are easy to eat and unlikely to be messy. Avoid soups, which may spill, or spaghetti, which requires attention to swirl and get into one's mouth without slurping. Boxed lunches with sandwiches or salads, carrot sticks or chips (though crunchy chips may be noisy), and cookies are easy for everyone. Pizza and soda attracts students at almost any time. Outside of mealtimes, faculty enjoy cheese and crackers, veggies, and water or coffee in the late afternoon. Wine can make the event special.

We were seeking to generate excitement about and interest in a new student learning plan as we also sought to learn what faculty saw as the most important areas in need of improvement. So, we invited all full-time faculty to focus group discussions—calling the event "Celebration & Conversation"—and offered wine and cheese and light but hot appetizers. Attendance was excellent as faculty were curious about the initiative, knew it was needed, saw the wine and cheese as festive, and were surprised at being offered something so delightful. The focus group discussions yielded the information needed and the wine and cheese along with upbeat presentations encouraged support for the initiative.

While food or high-quality snacks are always appreciated, full meals or the very best snacks are generally not necessary. Indeed, we have conducted faculty focus groups with bottled water and packaged cookies and chips. No one expects them and some participants take nothing while others open a package and have just a few bites. The important point is to show participants appreciation for their attendance and to offer them something to do with their hands at the beginning of the group in order to get comfortable.

Inviting and Reminding Participants

Invite participants once locations, dates, times, refreshments, and incentives have been scheduled, as this information should be included in the invitation to both inform and encourage participation. The contact method may vary by segment. E-mailing potential participants is the easiest and most inexpensive form of contact; however, other forms may be more appropriate based on the population. Social media has become a preferred method of engaging students, so a post there may be more effective than a targeted e-mail. If the segment is very specific, then in-person announcements at a meeting or lecture may be appropriate. An RSVP form should be included in the invitation along with the focus group purpose, location, time, day, incentives, and refreshments.

If running a number of groups per segment, consider offering participants the opportunity to specify their preferred and alternative time and day choices. This gives the researchers the ability to assign participants to a group in order to achieve the minimum number of participants (7) or avoid going over the maximum number (10). Remember that it is necessary to continually consider how many participants from each segment need to be invited to get a certain number of RSVPs, in order to have a certain number of participants actually show up. Web-based meeting management software like Doodle polls enable participants to check all of the times they might be available. And web-based survey tools like SurveyMonkey or Qualtrics enable the client, FG Expert, or Organizer to invite participants and collect RSVPs along with any other desired information.

Contact the participants one or two days before the date to remind them of the focus group details (including refreshments and incentives) and to confirm participation. This reminds the participants about their appointment and if they need to change, then the Organizer can inform the participant of alternative group dates if available or perhaps find a replacement participant.

Supplies

Each focus group requires a number of supplies easily transported to the location in a basket, box, or supply bag.

Moderator's Guides

Print three single-sided copies of the expanded Moderator's Guide for the moderators' use in facilitating the group and taking notes. The expanded Moderator's Guide contains each topic's questions at the top of the page with the rest of the page blank for easy note-taking.

Digital Recorders and Extra Batteries

Each supply bag should include two digital recorders. Both will be used during the group in case one fails. Make sure that the batteries are fully charged and that additional batteries are included in the supply bag. A recorder that is no longer working because the batteries died quickly becomes a distraction if one of the moderators must reach for and install new batteries. No matter what the other moderator says, everyone's attention becomes focused on the recorder.

The focus group may be videotaped if one-way glass is available. Note, though, that videotaping is much more resource-intensive, as it requires a special room, additional equipment, and a technician. Video also takes longer to analyze as the data are visual in addition to auditory. We have found that it is simply not worth the resources expended for the kinds of projects anticipated in this book.

Tent Cards and Markers

Tent cards with only first names are placed in front of each participant. These may be prepared in advance or participants may write their own names on them. Tent cards are not necessary if everyone knows one another, perhaps because they are an identifiable group that meets regularly such as the Associate Dean's Council.

Index Cards and Pens

Provide enough five-inch-by-eight-inch index cards in two different colors and pens for each participant. These will be used to collect responses to the warm-up and wrap-up questions. Using a different color for each question makes sorting easy. If you use two warm-up questions and one wrap-up question, then provide three different colors.

Thank You Gifts and Incentives

If distributing thank you gifts or incentives, be sure to include these in the supply bag. If there will be a drawing for an incentive, include whatever material will be used to draw names, such as small sheets of paper for participants to write their names and a hat or box from which names will be drawn.

Refreshments

The supply bag will include light refreshments if catering is not used.

Flip Chart With Easel Stand and Markers

If you wish to write questions or responses on a board to focus attention during the discussion or to brainstorm recommendations, bring along a flip chart with easel stand and markers. Self-stick easel pads with adhesive backs are particularly easy to use as they do not require a cumbersome stand, can be rolled up for easy carrying, and will stay put on the wall without tape.

Phone Numbers

Include the cell phone numbers of all moderators and the Organizer in case of any emergency. Also include the number for catering in case they appear to be delayed.

Setting Up and Welcoming Participants

Late in the day before or a few hours prior to the group, the Organizer should make certain that the room is correctly set up with a conference table and chairs, and a separate table for food or snacks and drinks. At least 30 minutes in advance of the group, the Organizer should arrive with all of the required supplies. If a meal is provided, make certain that catering arrives as scheduled so they are gone before participants arrive.

The moderators should arrive about 15 to 20 minutes prior to the start of the group. The Organizer will show them the supplies and confirm that they are prepared to conduct the group. The moderators will sit across from each other at the table, so they should place personal items and name cards in appropriate places. The most experienced moderator should sit closest to the door so he or she can prevent any late arriver from entering.

If conducting several groups at once, the Organizer should set up and staff a table outside of the main entrance for check-in and to welcome and direct participants. For a single group the moderators can welcome participants, thereby freeing the Organizer to return to other responsibilities.

Greet and welcome participants and note their attendance. Make them feel comfortable and appreciated with small talk and point out the location of the restrooms. If serving food, invite them to go through the buffet or grab a boxed meal and begin eating. This saves time both in the food line and in actually consuming the meal.

When it's time to begin, the moderators should go to their seats if not already there, call the group together, and either offer greetings from the appropriate stakeholders who initiated the focus group or introduce one representative who will thank the participants and relate the importance of their presence. That person should then leave, as our new provost did, so that the focus group may begin.

> Within six weeks of his arrival, the new provost requested that we conduct focus groups to help him learn about the campus. He had already identified several constituencies from whom he wished to hear and the questions he wanted asked. We collaborated to make a few modifications and then got to work. The provost came to the beginning of each group and thanked the participants for sharing their time and expertise, saying that they were giving him "a great gift" as he sought to understand the university's culture and faculty life, and mentioned that he hoped they enjoyed the food. His presence and these words alone earned him much goodwill as participants knew that his time was tight; they appreciated that he came to them to explain what he wanted and why, and that he paid for a meal. Participants expressed that the provost seemed very sincere in his expressions of gratitude. The discussions among those present and their comments were unusually frank and hopeful.

During the Focus Groups

Once the focus groups begin, the Organizer's responsibilities differ depending on whether there is only one group or more. If several focus groups are being conducted simultaneously, the Organizer should remain available outside of the rooms to answer any questions or deal with any problems. The Organizer will also prevent late arrivers from joining the group once introductions are completed, usually less than 10 minutes following the start of the group.

When only 10 to 15 minutes remain, the Organizer may also quietly enter the room and signal a reminder to the moderators that it is time to begin to close the group. This latter task is most useful to new moderators; seasoned moderators will be conscious of the time. As the groups conclude and participants leave, the Organizer will thank them and answer any remaining questions. Finally, once all participants have left, the Organizer will pick up remaining supplies and return the room to its original state.

If only a single group is in session the Organizer may focus on other duties for an hour and return about 15 minutes before the group ends to help return the room to its proper state and collect supplies. Or, moderators can take on these tasks and return the supply bag to the Organizer. A copy of the Logistics Checklist can be found in Appendix O.

James Vignette (Access)

Recall that the FG Expert asked James to review and confirm the logistics required to run successful focus groups—offering incentives, inviting the participants and sending reminders, choosing rooms for the focus groups, ordering food and beverages for the participants, and ordering any supplies that might be needed. Among all of these decisions, the most important might be choosing rooms where participants from underrepresented groups would feel most comfortable. Should the focus groups be conducted in the student center where many students come and go or in an office building where the participants could attend with greater anonymity? We have found working around an appropriately sized conference table to be the most comfortable setting, but perhaps this group will work better in a different setting. Beyond the intrinsic reward of helping oneself and others from similar backgrounds, what incentives might be offered? Perhaps money added to their student ID would help students to buy books and supplies or coffee or a meal. Can we get students' cell phone numbers so that we can call or text them reminders to attend the focus group?

FG Expert: "How are your plans for the focus groups coming, James? Have you chosen rooms for the focus groups and ordered food and supplies?"

James: "I think we have covered most everything, but it will be good to review our plans with you and get some feedback. We identified several small conference and seminar rooms in a couple of classroom buildings where we think students can come and go in relative anonymity as if they were attending a class. All have conference-type tables with chairs for 10 to 12 persons—10 participants and 2 moderators."

FG Expert: "Sounds good, James. Do the rooms have a side table or room for another table for snacks and drinks? What have you decided about food and drinks?"

James: "Yes, all rooms have tables or space for tables. And we have ordered sodas, water, cookies, and fruit from catering—nothing fancy. Hope that is okay."

FG Expert: "That sounds fine. We just want participants to feel appreciated. What about incentives?"

James: "Incentives are a bit challenging these days with tight budgets and fairly strict policies about paying students. Nevertheless, we think we can give them each $5 credit on their student ID that they can use in the cafeteria, food court, bookstore, or tech store. And they will be entered into a drawing for a $50 credit that one person will receive. So, there is a relatively good chance of winning the drawing."

FG Expert: "Well done, James; sounds like you have most everything in order. How many participants have RSVP'd? . . ."

The conversation continues until James and the FG Expert have discussed the logistics that need to be considered and implemented. Typically, there is a lot of concern about attracting enough students to attend the focus groups. The key seems to be having a compelling topic that is of concern to the participants, identifying the right participants, and having some flexibility in the scheduling of the groups. We have learned that it is not possible to invite participants, ask them for available dates and times, and then schedule the focus groups to accommodate their schedules. Instead we set the dates, times, and places, paying attention to classes and other events on the institution calendar to the extent possible. Occasionally, it works out to schedule the focus groups around another event that many of the participants will be attending. We usually set up more groups than needed, ask students to rank their top three choices, and then assign participants ideally to their first or second choice and cancel groups that few can attend. We typically will not run a focus group with fewer than four or five participants attending. And as we get down to four or five participants, we will sometimes decide to use just one moderator so as not to overwhelm the group.

Chris Vignette (Affordability)

Recall that the FG Expert asked Chris and the committee to work on and double-check the logistics of how they will conduct the focus groups— sending invitations and tracking RSVPs, reserving rooms and ordering food, identifying and purchasing incentives, and so on, as itemized on the checklist. Chris and the FG Expert agree to meet a few days before the focus groups to review their checklist of logistics.

Chris: "Wow, attending to logistics is a lot of work; a lot of details!"

FG Expert: "It is a lot of detailed but important work because we want to make sure that both our moderators and participants are comfortable and free from distractions so they can relax and participate fully in the conversation. So, are there any particular concerns or issues we need to discuss?"

Chris: "The most critical is how do we know who and how many participants will actually show up? How do we get comfortable with that?"

FG Expert: "You don't get comfortable with it. You keep asking if there is anything else that needs to be or can be done. Remember the primary question is how many students we need to invite to make sure that a certain number RSVP in order to make sure that 9 to 10 participants actually attend. I know how many you invited; how many RSVP'd that they would attend? And what is your plan for reminding them?"

Chris: "We canceled a few groups and merged the participants in with other groups so that we now have at least 6 registered participants for each of the 12 groups."

FG Expert: "And you are not entirely comfortable with that? What incentives are you offering? Is everyone familiar with and able to discuss the topic for 60 minutes or so? What kind of food have you ordered? When and where are the focus groups scheduled?"

Chris: "I think we have covered all of those details to the best of our ability. But what do we do if only three or four students show up?"

FG Expert: "That is probably our greatest fear in conducting focus groups, particularly focus groups with students, Chris. Do you have a plan for sending reminder e-mails or text messages?"

Chris: "Yes, we will be sending reminder texts both on the day before and the day of their scheduled group. And we will ask them to confirm or tell us if they can no longer attend."

FG Expert: "Excellent, Chris. Now it comes down to deciding at what point it is no longer a group but more of a group interview that is likely to become a question-and-answer session rather than a discussion among participants. And do we need co-moderators to conduct the group or would that be too overwhelming? We typically discuss our options before the focus groups begin and have a plan in place, but it ultimately comes down to professional judgment when it is time to begin the group."

The conversation continues until they have covered all of Chris's questions and the checklist. The FG Expert makes a few suggestions, which stimulates Chris's thinking and leads to some other ideas. As they conclude their meeting, the FG Expert asks Chris to talk with the committee and their stakeholders to confirm the type of report the committee would prefer.

8

STEP #6: ANALYZE THE DATA AND REPORT THE RESULTS

So What Does It All Mean?

Analyzing focus group data using the ODU Method is a multistep process with built-in redundancies to ensure the consistency and accuracy of the results. This chapter explains the process in detail. Once again, a complete Moderator's Guide and well-trained moderators are key, as it is the moderators, using the guide, who provide much of the labor in data analysis. The Moderator's Guide serves as the template for analysis and is used by the moderators individually to prepare their reports; the two co-moderators of each group then meet and review each other's report and prepare a co-moderator report. The FG Expert then reviews all of the reports and holds a debriefing for all moderators prior to preparing the Final Report. The results are confirmed in a town hall format open to all participants plus the entire segment of the community. This final step emphasizes the "listening and learning" purpose of focus groups in higher education, and the town hall format demonstrates the ability of focus groups to build community and encourage buy-in to the results and the answers or solutions that flow from them.

Shirley: "Now that the focus groups have begun and are progressing well, can we talk again about the data analyses and what the report will look like?"

FG Expert: "Sure. What were you anticipating and what are your committee and your stakeholders expecting?"

Shirley: "I was assuming transcripts of the focus groups plus thematic analyses, a summary, and recommendations. However, as I recall you mentioned another method that you and your team have developed. When I discussed your plan with my team, however, several of our more quantitatively oriented faculty and even one of the more qualitatively oriented faculty had questions about its reliability and validity."

FG Expert: "We work a little differently because of the resources we have in higher education and the types of decisions we are trying to inform. We are not seeking statistical significance or making critical decisions based on our analyses. We are merely trying to make some improvements in the university's retention rates. So, in qualitative focus group research we are typically looking for consistency rather than reliability, and accuracy and trustworthiness instead of validity."

Shirley: "I agree, but some of those programs designed to improve retention rates can also be expensive."

FG Expert: "Indeed, but these focus groups are not so much designed to offer recommendations for specific interventions. If we do our job well, we will have clearly identified the problems and related issues in some depth and from that some broad suggestions for interventions will emerge. Those data and the recommendations should inform your committee as they proceed to make recommendations for more specific initiatives. And you can always follow up with some town hall meetings among the same segments we identified for the focus groups. Or you could follow up with a survey asking for input from the community about specific initiatives."

Shirley: "Good points, as always! So, can you review your analysis plans with me once more? And perhaps attend my next committee meeting?"

FG Expert: "Certainly. As a first step we ask the moderators to complete the initial analyses individually using the Moderator's Guide and adding bullet points for the themes they have identified listening to the recording and reviewing their notes. The moderators are faculty and administrators who are well-educated people who have been trained how to lead discussions and conduct research. They are also familiar with the culture of the university. I know, and our experience confirms, that they can identify emerging themes without doing all of the customary transcription."

Shirley: "Then what?"

FG Expert: "After each moderator has completed his or her individual analyses and typed bulleted themes for each topic into a copy of the Moderator's Guide, the second step is to ask the co-moderators to meet and discuss their findings question by question. Thus, they are checking the accuracy of their findings against each other. They may have similar observations and some contradictory observations, which they discuss, and as necessary they refer back to the recording and their notes. Typically, they come to consensus fairly easily, and if not, they include both points of view to bring forward to the next step. Based on their discussions, they submit a combined report to us."

Shirley: "So then we have several different reports to review?"

FG Expert: "Right, and the third step is to bring all the moderators who facilitated groups from the same segments together for a modified focus group so we do not generalize across different segments. For instance, we would not want to mix the moderators who worked with the faculty with the moderators who worked with students. We all have an opportunity to review the reports submitted by each pair of co-moderators, and we basically go through the Moderator's Guide question by question and engage the co-moderators in a discussion about their findings, looking for both commonalities and differences. We discuss until we have agreement on a segment report."

Shirley: "So now we have four reports, one from each segment: currently enrolled students who returned in academic difficulty, currently enrolled students who returned in academic success, faculty, and advisers."

FG Expert: "Correct. Then we have to decide, based on what you and your committee desire, whether to attempt to bring all of these reports together into one report OR whether it is better to keep them separate and look for commonalities and differences. We also need to discuss what you and the stakeholders want the report to look like. Is a copy of the Moderator's Guide with bulleted themes sufficient or would you prefer a full written report? Perhaps you should discuss this with your committee and other stakeholders."

Analyzing the Data

As noted previously in our discussion with Shirley, higher education's human capital resources in the form of educated faculty and staff make focus groups a feasible choice for seeking in-depth information. Trained moderators can review their notes and listen to recordings and do not need expensive transcriptions in order to identify themes. Most faculty and administrators have master's and doctoral degrees and have taken (and perhaps taught) several research courses. Most have also conducted, or at least participated in, some type of research. They understand methodology and the importance of following protocols.

Regardless of discipline and based on their professional experiences, most faculty and administrators also know how to lead good group discussions. Our experience is that faculty and administrators can become very good moderators with a little training. The same is true of many graduate students who are in the middle of their education and often eager to enhance their skills and gain valuable experience to include on their vitae. And in certain circumstances, undergraduate students can be trained if there are particular focus groups we feel comfortable with them moderating. While some obvious disciplinary differences among faculty exist, we have worked successfully with faculty in the sciences, the humanities, professional schools (business, engineering, education, health sciences), and the social sciences. We have also found that there is now greater acceptance of the consistency and accuracy of qualitative research; even many of our more quantitatively oriented faculty and administrators quickly become comfortable with the focus group process and accept its value as a rigorous methodology. Obviously, we choose moderators based on more than just degrees and experience; we need to know about their interpersonal skills (discussed in chapter 6). We typically have worked with most of them and observed how well they work with others. We have also interviewed those whom we do not know but who have been referred by another moderator.

Data analyses are completed to answer each research question and address the purpose of the focus group. Because the topic questions in the Moderator's Guide are derived from the research questions, analyzing the answers to the topic questions should answer the research questions that were designed to address the purpose. Thus, we begin with the Moderator's Guide as a template. Typically, we edit the Moderator's Guide to take out most of the instructions and prompts so as to leave only the purpose statement, warm-up and wrap-up questions, and actual topic questions, and then distribute these to the moderators electronically. The moderators open their copies of this document and begin by typing verbatim all of the answers to the warm-up and wrap-up questions. We encourage them to enclose the comments in quotation marks and not correct the grammar or punctuation. They can then use markers or highlighting within the software to identify themes. The moderators are also asked to include a listing or chart of the group by race or ethnicity and gender or any other critical demographic factors to ensure appropriate diversity.

Moderators then listen to the digital recording. Rather than summarizing the focus group discussions in general, the moderators are encouraged to listen for emerging themes for each individual question both when listening and taking notes during the discussion and when listening to the recording. What are the three or four predominant themes of the discussion for each question? How many of the other participants agreed with each theme either verbally or nonverbally? How many disagreed? Was there some final consensus or was there a debate that needs to be reported? Moderators are encouraged not to include as themes statements made by one person without any comment or acknowledgment from the other participants, regardless of how compelling it may sound. The emerging themes do not need to be written in complete sentences and could as easily be listed as bullet points. Moderators also look for themes from participants that might be stated differently but are essentially addressing the same point. It is also important for moderators to notice what is *not* mentioned that was expected to be. For example, in a Quality of University Life focus group discussing campus safety, what does it mean if no one mentions lighting as an issue or the escort service as an initiative designed to protect students, faculty, and staff, especially if these were relatively recent, expensive, and well-advertised initiatives? And finally, moderators are encouraged to identify short, direct quotations that capture a particular point made in the discussion. The quotations should be included without attribution to protect the confidentiality of the participants. For example, in one staff focus group for the new president, the discussion of infrastructure led one participant to say, "Now even the support staff need support staff." While a great quote in itself, we included it in the final report because it perfectly expressed the prevalent and recurring theme that work expectations had increased dramatically without concomitant increases in the number of staff.

The focus group methodology described here is designed to enhance consistency through the use of a Moderator's Guide and moderator training to make sure that everyone uses the Moderator's Guide in the same manner. As a part of data analysis we check the accuracy of the data by comparing analyses among moderators. As a first step, moderators review their own notes and listen to the recording of their focus group to identify emerging themes that they add to the template based on the Moderator's Guide. Co-moderators then exchange reports and compare notes to check their individual analyses against each other and again listen to the recording as necessary. They review, discuss, agree, or disagree and record common themes into one report for their focus group.

A second step to check the accuracy of the data is to conduct a debriefing (focus group) among all of the moderators who moderated a focus group in a particular segment. The FG Expert distributes reports from each focus group to all of the moderators involved and then proceeds through the Moderator's Guide question by question, engaging the moderators in a discussion about the results, much as was done in the actual focus group. Ultimately, a consensus is reached among the moderators and the data are incorporated into one report using the template developed from the Moderator's Guide. The final report for each segment looks much like the original individual moderator reports, although it is likely more extensive.

The ultimate method for checking the accuracy of the data is to get feedback from the focus group participants and others who are members of the segment but did not participate in a focus group. We typically try to conduct town hall meetings within each segment, during which we present the data and ask for feedback. We report faculty data through a meeting of the faculty senate, administrator data through a meeting of their constituency group, and student data through the student senate. Creswell (2014) calls this *member checking*. When their responses are positive—that is, when they affirm that the results make sense to them and reflect their perceptions—we are confident in the analyses and ready for the final report.

If there is fine-tuning to be done, the FG Expert does that. And if there is little consensus on the accuracy of the data, we would consider running one or two more focus groups in that segment. We may include town hall comments and feedback in the report as additional data. Because these data occurred outside of the group discussion and were not debated as they might have been in the group, they are not integrated into the main results. They are additional but different data and should be treated as such. We thus avoid altering the report significantly except for corrections and clarifications.

Reporting the Results

After all of the data are analyzed and individual segment reports are written, it is time to contact Shirley and her committee to discuss whether they prefer to receive the individual segment reports or one overall report based on common themes across segments. Each has advantages and challenges and the choice should be informed by the purpose statement and research questions as well as the stakeholders. Are the stakeholders expecting institution-wide interventions or initiatives or are they expecting to consider interventions and initiatives for each segment? In general, looking for common themes across all segments is more likely to suggest institution-wide initiatives to improve student success, although the initiatives will be different or the roles they play in implementing them will vary among faculty, administrators, and students. Segment reports provide information about how best to work with each group. The challenges include the time required to develop the individual reports and the resources available to provide multiple initiatives.

It is now time to discuss with Shirley what the report should look like.

FG Expert: "Shirley, we are almost finished drafting the four segment reports. How would you like to proceed from here? Would you like to host some town hall meetings to verify our analyses? What would you like the report to look like?"

Shirley: "I think we would like to do three town hall meetings; one each with the faculty senate, the student senate, and all of the advisers. What would those look like? Who hosts them? And who reports the data?"

FG Expert: "Typically, we ask the leadership of the senate and the other two associations to invite their constituents to a regularly scheduled open meeting or to call a special meeting expressly for the purpose of reviewing and responding to the data. You and your committee are welcome to report the data or we will be happy to do so. You will want to summarize the data in the first half of the meeting and devote at least half of the time to listening to questions and comments so we can get a sense of how accurate they perceive our results to be."

Shirley: "Great—let's co-present the data and I will ask our committee to take some notes. I am assuming PowerPoint will work."

FG Expert: "PowerPoint is fine as long as we do not fill up the slides with data and then read the slides to the participants. We can also distribute five-inch-by-eight-inch cards toward the end of the session and invite participants to respond to the wrap-up question we used in the focus groups. We must keep those separate, however. But they frequently generate some interesting data and keep everyone involved and committed. What do you want the final report to look like?"

Shirley: "If you can create a one- to two-page Executive Summary and add the four segment reports as appendices, that will suffice for now. However, our committee would like to meet with you to discuss the results along with possible overlapping themes. I will set up the town hall meetings if you will draft the Executive Summary and create a PowerPoint template for us that you think would be a good way to display the data."

FG Expert: "I will draft a report and add the Research Proposal we used. This will outline the purpose of the focus groups and the research questions we were addressing. One last thing to consider: The town hall meetings will help to make the data available to the constituents. However, many will not be able to attend and there will not be any recommendations included in the town hall meetings. What is your plan for disseminating these results plus recommendations to the individual constituencies and the campus community?"

Shirley: "I have not thought much about that. Let me talk with the team and develop a plan for disseminating the results and recommendations. I'll get back to you."

FG Expert: "Just one final comment, Shirley: We always recommend to clients that they act on some recommendation very visibly and fairly quickly so that all of the participants and others who know about the focus group project know that you have listened to them."

As can be seen from our discussion with Shirley, once the data are analyzed there are several decisions that need to be made about how best to report it to different stakeholders. We have never encountered any stakeholder who wanted a full formal written report. All have been quite satisfied with bulleted thematic reports following the format of the Moderator's Guides and relevant parts of the Research Proposal. Some may want recommendations as well, and some may prefer to develop their own recommendations based on the data. Unless the Moderator's Guide includes questions about recommendations so that they are part of the data, it is best to let the client develop the recommendations based on their review of the data along with their knowledge of the circumstances that led to the focus groups. Remember that they are the content experts about their constituency.

Finally, as we informed Shirley, participants and others who know about the focus groups are always curious to hear about the results and recommendations. Some may also be a little skeptical about whether or not they will hear all of the findings, both good and bad. While the town hall meetings help to report the results, many constituents are not able to attend, and typically, the recommendations are not yet developed. We encourage clients to publish at least an Executive Summary of the report on the website and implement even a small change or recommendation as soon as possible to tell people their voices have been heard and their feedback was valuable.

A copy of the moderators' thematic analysis is in Appendix M and the Final Report is in Appendix N.

James Vignette (Access)

Having resolved the logistical issues in chapter 7, it is now time to begin preparations for completing the data analyses and drafting the reports. The

FG Expert will discuss the data analysis process with James and ask him and his committee to decide what they would like the final report to look like based on the audiences to whom they want to present it. Will the typical analyses incorporated as bullet points into the Moderator's Guide suffice, or is a more detailed report needed for a particular constituency? Will there be an opportunity for town hall meetings to present the results to the participants along with other underrepresented group members to ask them to validate the results and offer some suggestions? To what extent does James want the FG Expert to assist in presenting the results to various constituencies? As we discovered in our vignette with Shirley, there are a lot of details to be covered, and some of them can make a difference between a very successful or moderately successful focus group project.

James: "The focus groups are well under way now, so it seems like a good time to review the logistics of analyzing and reporting the data. I know we want the co-moderators to be involved, but what are my instructions for them?"

FG Expert: "It is a good time to review this part of the Research Proposal, James. As you recall, we talked with the moderators about the data analysis process when we trained them. We want them to complete an individual thematic analysis within about a week after their focus group so it will still be fresh. We also want them to complete the analysis for the first group before they moderate a second group so as not to conflate the results. As I recall you agreed that using the Moderator's Guide as a template for their analyses would be a good format for your committee, right?"

James: "Yes, we think that using bullet points in the Moderator's Guide to discuss the themes will meet our needs very well. I assume that the moderators will also type in the data collected using five-inch-by-eight-inch cards to respond to the warm-up and wrap-up questions verbatim, right?"

FG Expert: "Right, and they will do a thematic analysis of those data as well. Then we will ask the co-moderators to meet and compare and contrast their results into one document to represent their focus group. We will then conduct a debriefing with all of the co-moderators for each constituency to create a report for that constituency."

James: "Right, and I have scheduled a date and time for that debriefing. Will you conduct that or am I supposed to do that?"

FG Expert: "How about if we do it together because you are the content expert and client while I am the FG Expert?"

James: "Great—anything else I should know or communicate to the moderators?"

FG Expert: "Let's see; just a few tips perhaps. Co-moderators should seek consensus on their themes, but they do not have to have absolute agreement on all of the themes in their combined report. They can report their different observations to the rest of the moderators for discussion and comparison to the data from the other group. Moderators should constantly ask themselves and each other, 'Is this something I heard from everyone or was this just one person's thought?' If they only heard one person say it but saw a lot of head nodding or heard other verbal agreements, it is probably a theme. Remind moderators to listen for what is not said as well as what is said. That is, is there something we might expect participants to say but no one did? That may be a finding as well."

James: "Great thoughts; anything else? And what about the town hall follow-up—what do you think about that? . . ."

The conversation continues as James and the FG Expert discuss how the data analysis will proceed and agree on a data analysis plan.

Chris Vignette (Affordability)

Chris and the committee have designed an ambitious project about an important topic. The FG Expert wants to meet with Chris to revisit and confirm their data analysis and reporting plan.

FG Expert: "Chris, I have reviewed your final Research Proposal, especially the part outlining the data analysis plan and report format. I assume that you and the committee have not changed those plans and we can proceed as planned."

Chris: "I am glad you called because this topic was recently discussed at the President's Cabinet. As you know some of them are more quantitatively oriented and want to be assured that these data will be reliable and valid so they can make data-based decisions about resolving whatever issues we find."

FG Expert: "Oh boy. These questions come up occasionally because qualitative research is still not widely understood or accepted. In short, the terms *reliability*, *validity*, and *statistical significance* are quantitative terms that do not apply to focus group data. Nor do the data analyses or the type of sampling used support quantitative decisions. That said, focus groups are a rigorous and relevant method for collecting the data to answer your research question. And they support data-based decision-making. We use a common Moderator's Guide and train the moderators to ask the questions in a consistent manner (qualitative reliability). We check and double-check the findings from each group and then each cohort to ensure accuracy and credibility (qualitative validity). And as a final measure we will member check the results by reporting the data back to the participants in town hall meetings and requesting their feedback, again to ensure accuracy and authenticity. Rather than reliability and validity, we talk about consistency and accuracy. What do you think? Will that satisfy them?"

Chris: "Wow, I hope so."

FG Expert: "Another thought is that we should start with the research questions: (a) What is the impact on student success of working while earning a college degree?; (b) Other than earning money, what is the benefit of working while attending college?; and (c) Is there a difference depending on whether students work on or off campus and how many hours per week they work? I would be happy to discuss the cabinet's concerns with them if you like."

Chris: "Great! I will try to set up a meeting with those who are most concerned. If they are in agreement, we are happy with the data analysis and reporting plan that we agreed on."

With the help of the FG Expert, Chris and the committee have developed a very good plan for conducting focus groups to answer their research questions and lead to discussions about how to improve the situation for students who are working while attending college. Now we cross our fingers and hope that all goes well. And we are prepared to address any challenges or problems as they arise.

9

THE BEST LAID PLANS

When to Just Say "No" or to Create
Plans B Through E

We have created a thorough Research Proposal and obsessed over the details, so what could possibly go wrong? As anyone in higher education knows, almost anything can go wrong in a big project, and something probably will. Good planning does help to prevent most problems and make those that do occur easier to resolve, but it does not resolve them all. We have learned that our response to the inevitable unexpected challenges is critical if there is to be any chance of salvaging the project. Occasionally, projects need to be postponed or canceled, but most often problems can be resolved and moved beyond to complete a credible focus group.

Problems can occur at any of the steps in the process:

1. Developing the Research Proposal
2. Selecting participants
3. Designing the Moderator's Guide
4. Selecting and training the moderators
5. Conducting the focus groups
6. Analyzing the data and reporting the results

Remember that conducting focus groups is not a linear process and the Research Proposal is a living document. With this in mind, problems in selecting participants, designing the Moderator's Guide, or selecting and training the moderators are a little easier to resolve. Simply revisit and revise the Research Proposal and the Moderator's Guide. However, creating a Research Proposal to which all stakeholders agree and presenting results that meet everyone's approval can be more difficult as the challenges often have to be confronted in the moment of the meeting with stakeholders. Probably the greatest fear people conducting focus groups have is what happens when something goes wrong during the focus group. Obviously, decisions must be made very quickly without much, if any, time to think or discuss.

This chapter covers a range of challenges and possible solutions. Fortunately, administrators and faculty are used to dealing with challenging people and situations and developing creative solutions.

When Asked to Do the Impossible

Consider three stories. A new president "asks" us to design and conduct full-day (six-hour) focus groups at the administrative retreat in two weeks, will not allow us to bring in trained moderators, wants to sit in on all of the focus groups, and wants us to present the data the next morning. Because we did such a good job, after we return to campus she "asks" us to conduct more focus groups with faculty, staff, and students in the next six weeks so she can report the data to the campus during her inauguration. Or how about this: The new provost "asks" us to conduct focus groups with samples of all academic affairs staff and report back to him in three weeks. Finally, a colleague with some authority, though not over us and not as much as the colleague thinks, pushes us to do focus groups but is not open to discussing whether or not focus groups are the best approach, or how they can be accomplished in the time expected. These are all true stories the authors have experienced.

The focus group process discussed in this book was developed through these and other experiences. We developed Research Proposals when the president requested focus groups; the project was high stakes and we needed clear communication and a common understanding among our Research Team and with the stakeholders (i.e., the president and her cabinet) about exactly how we planned to proceed. We also developed our Moderator's Training Guide then as we learned that we could not use any of our trained moderators at the administrative retreat; instead, we had to select and quickly train some of the staff who were already attending the retreat. We embraced the co-moderator model then upon realizing that some of the staff would not be comfortable moderating a group alone, especially a group lasting six hours. Because we had to analyze and report on the data from seven groups early the next day, we knew that two sets of notes and memories from each focus group would help, as would requesting written responses to warm-up and wrap-up questions. We also realized that it would be most expedient to complete the analyses using the Moderator's Guide as a template. However, designing the Moderator's Guide was deceptively easy because the president handed us eight questions that we could not change but were able to tweak a bit and organize so the conversation would flow smoothly.

Following another decade of experience conducting many focus groups, the challenge of meeting the provost's expectations was much easier. We were well prepared to negotiate some of the details with him. The first and perhaps most important detail was to convince him that he needed three more moderators to help co-moderate the groups, analyze the data, and write the reports. The provost also had a list of questions that were used by a well-known national expert in a survey. Once again we tweaked a few questions to make them open ended and organized them into a consistent and accurate Moderator's Guide.

When it is the president or provost who is asking for a focus group, "no" is probably not an option. We have found, however, that with a little creativity plus some good communication and a solid Research Proposal, the project can move forward with a few alterations that make it doable even if still difficult. There are other times when we can say "no," but doing so is difficult. Often these situations arise when someone makes a request for help conducting focus groups and perhaps even has an interesting topic, but the current proposal does not meet the criteria for focus groups or perhaps would likely not generate much discussion among participants. Some important questions that simply cannot be answered with focus groups include: Why don't some students use the library? Why do some students attend student affairs events? Simply put, the students with the answers to those questions are likely the very same students who will not respond to invitations to attend a focus group asking about them. Perhaps the best response to these requests is to ask clients how they think focus groups will work in this situation. The FG Expert can also work through the steps with them to help them to understand how their question does not fit the model or help them to modify their topic so that it does fit the model.

On rare occasions a client loses sight of reality about what it takes to conduct focus groups or the extent to which the topic is doable. Assuming the client is not the president or provost, the Research Team must accept the responsibility of their expertise, say "no," and walk away. If the client is the president or provost, the Team must write a clear Research Proposal that includes an outline of the limitations, complete the focus groups, and submit the report.

Challenges During the Planning Stages

Problems can also arise in selecting participants, designing the Moderator's Guide, or selecting and training the moderators. It is not uncommon, especially when working with students, to have difficulty getting participants to

RSVP or check their e-mail. Very few responses to an invitation indicate a potentially boring topic (at least to the population) or bad timing.

As we saw in the vignette with Chris, we are sometimes trying to sample specific groups about which we have no data in the student information system; for example, we do not know whether or not they are working off campus. So, it is important to go deeper into the population to sample more students or to create a survey with screening questions to help identify the population. We typically go through five or six revisions of a Moderator's Guide to make sure that it will lead to accurate and consistent data. Stakeholders and moderators edit the guide based on their knowledge, and in some situations we pilot test it with a sample of the population. After running an actual focus group, we may then ask the participants about each question in the guide. Do they understand the questions? Did participants interpret the question in the way we intended? Are their interpretations the manner in which the question was intended? We continually revise the Moderator's Guide and also revise the Research Proposal as needed.

Moderators may present another challenge. Some moderators may withdraw because they are not comfortable with the process, while others may turn out to be less capable than expected. During the moderator training session it may be possible to identify those who may not perform well; we often try to invite more people to the training than we may end up needing for this very reason. Unfortunately, we find out about others only after they conduct the focus group. Using co-moderators helps to address the deficiency of a single moderator. Perhaps the co-moderator can salvage the data from the group, and perhaps we have to run another group.

In short, most of these challenges can be resolved with some thoughtful consideration and discussion. But what happens if when presenting the proposal or report to a group of stakeholders the methodology is questioned or if something goes wrong during the focus group?

When the Focus Group Methodology Is Questioned

Stakeholders who are engaged in making critical evidence-based decisions that might involve thousands of dollars are often interested in quantitative analyses such as dashboards and metrics on which to base their decisions. When they ask us to gather data to inform a particular decision, they want to know that those data are "reliable and valid" or "statistically significant," as mentioned in the vignette with Chris (chapter 8). These questions may come up in response to the proposal and perhaps again in response to the report, often during meetings when the FG Expert or client is presenting the proposal or report. Anyone presenting any kind of data to stakeholders has likely encountered these situations.

We trust that we have given readers the knowledge needed to explain the differences between quantitative and qualitative research, between reliability and consistency, and between validity and accuracy (chapter 1). In short, explain as simply and patiently as possible without being condescending that the terms *reliability, validity,* and *statistical significance* refer to quantitative research and do not apply to focus group data. Further, and perhaps more importantly, describe how focus groups are a rigorous and relevant method for collecting data that will give deep insight. Explain the use of a common Moderator's Guide and training the moderators to ask the questions in a consistent (reliable) manner. Checking and double-checking the findings from each group and then each segment ensures accuracy and credibility (validity). And as a final measure, member checking the results by reporting the data back to the participants in town hall meetings and requesting their feedback provides further evidence of accuracy and consistency.

When Things Go Wrong During the Focus Group

Despite the most careful preparations, things will occasionally go wrong. Catering arrives late or not at all. Supplies are missing. A moderator does not show up. Unannounced construction begins outside the window. A fire alarm goes off. A pipe breaks and floods the building. Do not panic. When things go wrong, the moderators are the saviors. They remain calm and make decisions about how to proceed.

Some mishaps do not unduly interrupt the purpose of the focus group. If the audio recorders are missing or without batteries, the moderators can take more notes. If one moderator cannot make it, the other takes the group and does the best job possible. If catering arrives after the group has begun and it is a meal that participants counted on, direct them to set up quietly; if the group discussion is sensitive then direct catering to set up outside the room. If they don't show up at all, apologize profusely to the participants and, if necessary, buy their lunches at the cafeteria or send them a gift card and charge the bill to catering. Participants will understand and will not blame you.

If something about the room makes it difficult to continue the group, such as excessive noise, one moderator should investigate and ask if work can be stopped or conditions changed for an hour. If not and it is possible to continue, shorten the discussion. If a fire alarm or some other emergency occurs that requires the group to evacuate, the moderators must balance the time lost, participants' other responsibilities, and where in the Moderator's

Guide the group was and then decide to cancel the group or continue the discussion until the all clear signal.

Extreme situations may require canceling the group. If so, the moderators will express gratitude that everyone is safe, regret that the group was interrupted, and more gratitude for everyone's understanding. There is nothing to be done. The most important thing is to remain calm and relaxed and, to the extent possible, lighthearted. Along with the moderators, participants are disappointed but usually understanding. Their time and the topic are important to them but rarely life altering. Promise to contact everyone within the next few days with news of a reschedule or decision not to, and then follow through with that promise. Communicating with participants after inconveniencing them demonstrates respect, encourages sympathy, and enhances the likelihood of future participation.

Sometimes only a few participants show up to the focus group. We will run a group with four participants and co-moderators; if only two or three participants show up, we run the group with one moderator since using co-moderators in this instance may lead the participants to feel overwhelmed.

A Note on Late Arrivers

Late arrivers present particular challenges. The first several minutes of the group are devoted to information and instructions including the statement that everything said is confidential; another minute or so is devoted to introductions. The group then moves on to the warm-up question, which takes about 5 minutes before jumping into the first topic of discussion. Arriving after the group guidelines and first discussion have occurred interrupts the group dynamics that have been established during the first discussion. Participants entering at or after this point—usually about 10 minutes after the opening of the group—disrupt the flow of conversation and divert attention from the topic as they generally enter with apologies and explanations and then take a moment to find seats and get brought up to speed regarding what is happening. In short, they hijack the group, focus attention on themselves, and distract from the purpose of the gathering, whether or not this was their intention. They have also missed the group guidelines, introductions, and especially the commitment to confidentiality. Even if introductions are unnecessary because everyone knows one another, the discussion is already under way; if interrupted, valuable time is lost as the moderators seek to restart the conversation, and tensions could arise since others expended considerable energy to arrive on time.

So how does one stop a late arriver once the group has begun? If the client or FG Expert is present outside the door, they can prevent anyone from entering. If there is no one outside and a participant is missing, the moderator sitting closest to the door should be prepared to jump up and prevent a late arriver from entering by walking the person back out of the room and closing the door. The other moderator will continue the group.

Explaining to late arrivers why they may not enter requires diplomacy. Generally, they will be embarrassed, flustered, and full of apologies and explanations as they really wanted and tried to be on time but something unexpected came up. Listen carefully and compassionately, ask sincerely if they are really okay, and affirm how frustrated they must be. Thank them for making the effort despite the unexpected events. Then apologize and explain with infinite kindness that the group is already well under way and that their entry now would disrupt the group's flow and create discomfort; apologize again and say that you just cannot disturb the group process. Most late arrivers will understand, indicate embarrassment and disappointment, apologize, and then relish the time they have saved as they go on about their day. They might be disappointed if they had counted on the food, so offer to bring out a boxed meal or to fix them a plate. If they indicate great disappointment because they really had some things they wanted to convey, offer to contact them within a few days to give them an opportunity to answer the questions. On extraordinarily rare occasions late arrivers may become quarrelsome, but hold your ground. In these cases insist again that you are happy to interview them so their responses may be included in the report. The following are two examples of late arrival.

Late arrivers nearly disrupted two different focus groups. In one case the late arriver understood not being able to enter but expressed dismay about missing lunch. When the moderator offered to bring out a boxed lunch, the late arriver was grateful, and the moderator returned to the room to retrieve a lunch and gave it to the person, who then left. The other case involved a participant whose assistant had contacted the FG Expert the day before saying that the person would be "a few minutes late." Thirty-five minutes into the group the late arriver opened the door, and the nearest moderator jumped up and walked the person back out of the room, explaining that it was too late to enter. The late arriver was upset, maintained that the Organizer had been informed of the late arrival, and insisted to be allowed entry. The moderator exhibited a remarkable degree of tact, explaining again why the group process was important and appealing to the late arriver's own research training with respect to the importance of following protocol and offering again to conduct an interview. At this point the late arriver threatened to go to the moderator's boss. The moderator held firm, and the late arriver left and did, in fact, head directly to the boss. The boss listened, apologized, and later called the moderator and asked that an interview with the late arriver be conducted; it was and the responses that echoed those of the group were included. No one was fired, and the boss quickly forgot the incident and later affirmed that all had ended well.

As we have all learned in higher education, things go wrong and the outcome depends on our calm, diplomatic, and thoughtful approach to the problem. As noted in this chapter, some problems or challenges are just part of the process and can be resolved by editing the Research Proposal or the Moderator's Guide or changing our process for sampling participants or selecting moderators. As mentioned before, the focus group methodology is not a linear process but resembles a spiral in which we cycle forward and backward through the steps or the Research Proposal. We have also learned in this book how to deal with some of the common and not-so-common challenges.

In Conclusion

Focus groups are confidential group discussions with a trained and skilled moderator using open-ended questions that promote interaction in order to explore participants' perspectives and experiences in a structured but relaxed atmosphere. Focus groups are a rigorous and relevant methodology organized around listening to and learning from participants that provides consistent and accurate data for use in leading institutions of higher education. Because they involve stakeholders, focus groups inform decision-making to shape policies and practices, build community, and increase participants' sense of value and commitment to the institution. Colleges and universities that want to employ focus groups are uniquely positioned because they are rich in the skilled human resources necessary to carry them out. We trust that *Using Focus Groups to Listen, Learn, and Lead in Higher Education* provides a valuable resource as we all work to address the big and small questions that confront our institutions and as we seek to improve the human capacity of our students and community.

Research Proposal Template

Focus Group Research Proposal

*[**Purpose**: To provide sufficient details about the focus group project to the focus group expert, moderators, and stakeholders to ensure that the project is a success. This section introduces the proposal by briefly describing the topic and what is hoped to be learned from the focus groups.]*
*[**Questions**: What is the importance of this topic to the organization? How do you know that it is important enough to potential participants to generate 60 to 90 minutes of discussion among the participants?]*

Focus Group Team

*[**Purpose**: To identify both the content experts who requested the focus group project and the consultants who have expertise in conducting focus groups.]*
*[**Questions**: Who are the content experts (e.g., clients)? Who are the focus group experts?]*

Name, Affiliation
Name, Affiliation

Purpose and Research Questions

*[**Purpose**: To state the overall purpose for the project followed by more specific research questions that become the topics for discussion during the focus groups.]*
*[**Questions**: What is the broad purpose? What are the more specific research questions?]*

The purposes of the research project are to learn about: (a) _____ and (b) _____. More specifically, the research questions are:

1. _____?
2. _____?
3. _____?
4. _____?

Participants

*[**Purpose**: To describe the large group from whom you will select a smaller sample to invite to participate in the focus groups and to describe that sample.]*

Population

*[**Questions**: What is the size of the large group/population? What are some of their important characteristics such as gender, race, and ethnicity as they pertain to the project?]*

Segments

*[**Questions**: Are there any segments of the population that might have different attitudes or opinions about the topic that should participate separately? Remember that focus groups are typically conducted with homogeneous groups.]*

Sample

*[**Question**: How many members of the population do you need to invite to get how many to respond to get 7 to 10 to attend? What are their characteristics? How will they be chosen?]*

Moderators

*[**Purpose**: To describe the process for selecting co-moderators who are appropriate for the topic and working with the participants in the focus groups along with their desired characteristics.]*
*[**Questions**: Remember that each focus group requires two moderators who will co-moderate a group. How many co-moderator teams will be used? How will they be chosen? What are their general qualifications and experience with focus groups? What is their relationship with participants?]*

All trained moderators will be invited to participate and subsequently chosen by the focus group team; teams of two moderators per group, preferably of different gender, race/ethnicity, or age, will co-moderate the groups.

Moderator's Guide

*[**Purpose**: To describe the purpose and content of the Moderator's Guide.]*

*[**Questions**: What are the topics included in the Moderator's Guide? How are they related to the research questions? What are the warm-up and wrap-up questions?]*

The Moderator's Guide includes a warm-up question, followed by questions covering four to six topics, and a wrap-up question. The complete Moderator's Guide follows this Research Proposal.

Logistics

*[**Purpose**: To describe all of the logistical details required to conduct the focus groups.]*
*[**Question**: WHAT needs to be done WHEN by WHOM?]*

- How many focus groups of 7 to 10 participants each are needed?
- What is the date, time, and place for conducting the focus groups?
- Who will send the invitation? E-mail or USPS? Will there be an RSVP, and if so, will it be via mail or using a web-based RSVP? Will the groups be first come, first served? Who will contact people a few days before the focus group to confirm their participation (i.e., reminder)?
- Who will greet and welcome the participants?
- Will refreshments (coffee, soda, water, cookies, fruit) be served or will a meal be served?
- Will there be incentives? If so, for each participant or one per group based on a random drawing?
- What materials will be needed—recorders, tent cards or name tags, markers, newsprint, five-inch-by-eight-inch cards, pens, and so on?

Data Analysis

*[**Purpose**: To identify who will be responsible for analyzing the data, how it will be analyzed, and how it will be reported.]*
*[**Questions**: Who will be responsible for analyzing and reporting the data? How will that be done? What will the report look like?]*

The focus group team will debrief the moderators within three weeks and then develop the report. The data analysis process includes three stages during which the co-moderators and focus group team review their notes and recordings and have conversations to identify emerging patterns and themes.

- Co-moderators individually review their notes and listen to the recording to produce bulleted themes that are typed into the Moderator's Guide.
- Co-moderators meet to compare and discuss their individual analyses and develop a combined analysis of bulleted themes that are typed into the Moderator's Guide and copied for the focus group team and other co-moderators.
- The focus group team debriefs all of the co-moderators in a segment using the Moderator's Guide.
- The focus group team will create the report based on the Moderator's Guide and the information in this proposal.

Time Line

*[**Purpose**: To present the time line for developing and conducting the focus groups and reporting the results.]*
*[**Questions**: Working backward from the date when the report is expected, when will the focus groups be conducted? When will the moderators be selected? When will the Moderator's Guide be developed? When will this Research Proposal be approved?]*

Costs

*[**Purpose**: To predict the costs involved in conducting the focus groups.]*
*[**Question**: What is the projected cost for each of the following items?]*

Incentives to participants (mugs, bookmarks, movie tickets)	$_____
Refreshments/meal for participants and moderators	$_____
Supplies: markers, cards, newsprint, tent cards/name tags	$_____
Printing and postage for invitations if mailed	$_____
Co-moderators	$_____
Consultants, if any	$_____
Total	$_____

Research Proposal Example: First-Year Student Success (Accountability)

Focus Group Team

Shirley Dankerdes, Vice President, Student Affairs (Client)
Jean Morris, Institutional Effectiveness and Assessment
Jim Watson, Institutional Effectiveness and Assessment
Stephen Calliotte, Student Affairs Assessment

Purpose and Research Questions

The purpose of the research project is to learn about the reasons students return after their first year. More specifically, the research questions are:

- What factors influence first-year students' decision to stay at an institution?
- What are first-year students' perceptions of their experiences?
- What factors contributed to first-year students' success?

Participants

Population

- Members of the first-year cohort who returned for their second year (fall 2015 cohort)
- Faculty teaching courses with high first-year enrollments
- Advisers of first-year students

Sample

- First-year students: randomly select 25% of the fall 2015 cohort
- Faculty: randomly select 50% of the population (about 100 faculty across the institution)
- Advisers: invite the whole population (about 30 advisers across the institution)

Moderators

The moderators for these groups will be a mix of midlevel administrators, faculty, and graduate students. All moderators are people with interpersonal skills who can facilitate a conversation with faculty, advisers, and students and who can conduct social science research or are focus group experts. There will be two moderators (co-moderators) per group with racial/ethnic, age, and gender diversity.

- First-year students who returned after their first year (fall 2015 cohort)
  o Co-moderators: higher education PhD student and Office of Assessment staff member
- Faculty teaching courses with high first-year enrollments
  o Co-moderators: full-time faculty member (lecturer or tenured) and administrator from a student support office
- Advisers of first-year students
  o Co-moderators: director of student success and Office of Assessment staff member

Moderator's Guide

The Moderator's Guide includes a warm-up question, followed by questions covering four topics, and a wrap-up question. The complete Moderator's Guide follows this Research Proposal.

Logistics

❖ How many focus groups of 7 to 10 participants each are needed?
- First-year students who returned after their first year (fall 2015 cohort)
  o Randomly sample 25% of the first-year class (about 250)
  o Invite all 250 students to participate in 1 of 2 groups
  o Accept 13 students per group
- Faculty teaching courses with high first-year enrollments
  o Randomly sample 50% of faculty teaching courses with high first-year student enrollments (about 100)
  o Invite all 100 to participate in 1 of 2 groups
  o Accept 10 faculty members per group
- Advisers of first-year students

o Invite 30 advisers to participate in 1 of 2 groups
o Accept 10 advisers per group

❖ What is the date, time, and place for conducting the focus groups? Times and days selected accommodate the university calendar and take place during times when either no classes are scheduled or early or late in the day.

- First-year students: Tuesday, March 15, 12:30–2:00 p.m. and Thursday, March 24, 5:00–6:30 p.m.
- Faculty: Tuesday, February 15, 3:00–4:30 p.m. and Friday, February 25, 8:30–10:00 a.m.
- Advisers: Tuesday, February 8, 8:30–10:00 a.m. and Thursday, February 10, 12:00–1:30 p.m.

❖ Who will send the invitation? E-mail or USPS? Will there be an RSVP and if so, will it be via mail or using a web-based RSVP? Will the groups be first come, first served? Who will contact people a few days before the focus group to confirm their participation (i.e., reminder)?

- Three weeks before each group is conducted, the Office of Assessment will send e-mail invitations to all selected samples with a link to RSVP for a group.
- A follow-up confirmation will be sent by the Office of Assessment seven days prior to the scheduled group.
- Phone calls confirming participation will be conducted by the Office of Assessment two days prior to the scheduled group.

❖ Who will greet and welcome the participants?

- First-year students: co-moderators
- Faculty: co-moderators and Shirley Dankerdes, vice president, student affairs
- Advisers: co-moderators and Shirley Dankerdes, vice president, student affairs

❖ Will there be refreshments served or will a meal be served?

- First-year students: pizza and soda
- Faculty: afternoon snacks and coffee for the afternoon group and breakfast for the morning group

- Advisers: lunch for the afternoon group and breakfast for the morning group

❖ Will there be incentives, and if so, for each participant or one per group based on a random drawing?

- First-year students: one participant in each group wins a pair of movie tickets
- Faculty: $5 gift card to campus coffee shop for all participants
- Advisers: $5 gift card to campus coffee shop for all participants

❖ What materials will be needed—recorders, tent cards or name tags, markers, newsprint, five-inch-by-eight-inch cards, pens, and so on?

- Two digital recorders per group
- Cardstock for name cards and markers per participant
- Two different color index cards per participant
- Pens per participant

Data Analysis

The focus group team will debrief the moderators within three weeks and then develop the report. The data analysis process includes three stages during which the co-moderators and focus group team review their notes and recordings and have conversations to identify emerging patterns and themes.

- Co-moderators individually review their notes and listen to the recording to produce bulleted themes that are typed into the Moderator's Guide.
- Co-moderators meet to compare and discuss their individual analyses and develop a combined analysis of bulleted themes that are typed into the Moderator's Guide and copied for the focus group team and other co-moderators.
- The focus group team debriefs all the co-moderators in a segment using the Moderator's Guide.
- The focus group team will create the report based on the Moderator's Guide and the information in this proposal.

Time Line

- Moderators will be selected and trained about two weeks prior to the first focus group.
- Focus groups will be conducted in February and March.
- The final report will be submitted to the vice president of student affairs by March 31.

Costs

Incentives to participants (mugs, bookmarks, movie tickets)	300
Refreshments/lunch for participants and moderators	1,000
Supplies: markers, five-inch-by-eight-inch cards, newsprint, tent cards/name tags	100
Printing and postage for invitations if mailed	0
Co-moderators ($50/group × 6 groups)	300
Consultants	0
Total	$1,700

Research Proposal Example: Increase Underrepresented Student Enrollment (Access)

Focus Group Team

James Castro, Director of Undergraduate Admissions (Client)
Jean Morris, Institutional Effectiveness and Assessment
Jim Watson, Institutional Effectiveness and Assessment
Stephen Calliotte, Student Affairs Assessment

Purpose and Research Questions

The purpose of the research project is to learn about how the institution can increase enrollments from underrepresented groups in higher education (U.S. citizens who are African American, Hispanic/Latino, or American Indian/Pacific Islander). More specifically, the research questions are:

- How important is it for students from underrepresented groups to attend college?
- How important is it for their families?
- What worries students from underrepresented groups about attending college?
- What can the faculty and staff do to help students from underrepresented groups to be successful both academically and socially?
- What are the chances students from underrepresented groups will be successful?

Participants

Population
- Currently enrolled students from underrepresented groups in higher education: U.S. citizens who are African American, Hispanic/Latino, or American Indian/Pacific Islander

Sample

- Two groups of underrepresented first-year students and two groups of underrepresented junior students
- Randomly select 20% from each group $N = 150$ first-year students/200 junior students

Moderators

The moderators for these groups will be a mix of midlevel administrators, faculty, and graduate students. All moderators are people with interpersonal skills who can facilitate a conversation with faculty, advisers, and students and conduct social science research, or are experts. There will be two moderators (co-moderators) per group with racial/ethnic, age, and gender diversity.

- Co-moderators: higher education PhD or criminal justice student, Office of Assessment staff member, or administrator from a student support office

Moderator's Guide

The Moderator's Guide includes a warm-up question, followed by questions covering three topics, and a wrap-up question. The complete Moderator's Guide follows this Research Proposal.

Logistics

❖ How many focus groups of 7 to 10 participants each are needed?
- Underrepresented groups of first-year and junior students
  o Randomly sample 20% of underrepresented students (first-year and junior)
  o Invite all students to participate in one of four groups
  o Accept 15 students per group
❖ What is the date, time, and place for conducting the focus groups? Times and days selected accommodate the university calendar and take place during times when either no classes are scheduled or early or late in the day.
- First-year students: Tuesday, March 15, 12:30–2:00 p.m. and Thursday, March 24, 5:00–6:30 p.m.

- Junior students: Tuesday, February 15, 3:00–4:30 p.m. and Friday, February 25, 11:00 a.m.–12:30 p.m.

❖ Who will send the invitation? E-mail or USPS? Will there be an RSVP, and if so, will it be via mail or using a web-based RSVP? Will the groups be first come, first served? Who will contact people a few days before the focus group to confirm their participation (i.e., reminder)?

  - Three weeks before each group is conducted, the Office of Assessment will send e-mail invitations to all selected samples with a link to RSVP with screening questions for a group.
  - A follow-up confirmation will be sent by the Office of Assessment seven days prior to the scheduled group.
  - Phone calls confirming participation will be conducted by the Office of Assessment two days prior to the scheduled group.

❖ Who will greet and welcome the participants?
  - Co-moderators

❖ Will there be refreshments served or will a meal be served?
  - Soda, water, cookies, and fruit

❖ Will there be incentives? If so, for each participant or one per group based on a random drawing?

  - For every student who shows up to the group: $5 credit on student ID card
  - Grand prize for each group: $50 credit on student ID card (one winner per group)

❖ What materials will be needed—recorders, tent cards or name tags, markers, newsprint, five-inch-by-eight-inch cards, pens, and so on?

  - Two digital recorders per group
  - Cardstock for name cards and markers per participant
  - Two different color index cards per participant
  - Pens per participant

Data Analysis

The focus group team will debrief the moderators within three weeks and then develop the report. The data analysis process includes three stages during which the co-moderators and focus group team review their notes and recordings and have conversations to identify emerging patterns and themes.

- Co-moderators individually review their notes and listen to the recording to produce bulleted themes that are typed into the Moderator's Guide.

- Co-moderators meet to compare and discuss their individual analyses and develop a combined analysis of bulleted themes that are typed into the Moderator's Guide and copied for the focus group team and other co-moderators.
- The focus group team debriefs all the co-moderators in this segment using the Moderator's Guide.
- The focus group team will create the report based on the Moderator's Guide and the information in this proposal.

Time Line

- Moderators will be selected and trained about two weeks prior to the first focus group.
- Focus groups will be conducted in February and March.
- The final report will be submitted to the director of undergraduate admissions by March 31.

Costs

Incentives to participants (mugs, bookmarks, movie tickets)	275
Refreshments/lunch for participants and moderators	750
Supplies: markers, five-inch-by-eight-inch cards, newsprint, tent cards/name tags	100
Printing and postage for invitations if mailed	0
Co-moderators ($50/group × 4 groups)	200
Consultants	0
Total	$1,325

Research Proposal Example: Impact of College Costs and Work on Student Success (Affordability)

Focus Group Team

Chris Meredith, Associate Vice President for Enrollment Management (Client)
Jean Morris, Institutional Effectiveness and Assessment
Jim Watson, Institutional Effectiveness and Assessment
Stephen Calliotte, Student Affairs Assessment

Purpose and Research Questions

The purpose of the research project is to learn about student perspectives on the value of college and the impact costs have on their success. Specifically, the research questions are:

- What is the cost of earning a college degree while incurring significant debt or spending many hours working?
- Other than earning money, what is the benefit of working while attending college?
- Is there a difference depending on whether students work on or off campus and how many hours per week they work?

Participants

Population
- Two groups of undergraduate students: first/second year and third/fourth year

Sample
- Representative sample of those who work on campus and those who work off campus based on screening questions asked as part of RSVP
- Randomly select 25% of first/second year and third/fourth year

Moderators

The moderators for these groups will be a mix of midlevel administrators, faculty, and graduate students. All moderators are people with interpersonal skills who can facilitate a conversation with faculty, advisers, and students, and who can conduct social science research or are focus group experts. There will be two moderators (co-moderators) per group with racial/ethnic, age, and/or gender diversity.

- Facilitated by higher education PhD or criminal justice student

Moderator's Guide

The Moderator's Guide includes a warm-up question, followed by questions covering three topics, and a wrap-up question. The complete Moderator's Guide follows this Research Proposal.

Logistics

❖ How many focus groups of 7 to 10 participants each are needed?
- First/second-year and third/fourth-year undergraduate students who work on and off campus
  - Multistage sampling
    - Randomly sample 20% of first/second-year and third/fourth-year undergraduate students (each)
    - Use a screening question to determine work status (on or off campus) and group assignment
❖ What is the date, time, and place for conducting the focus groups? Times and days selected accommodate the university calendar and take place during times when either no classes are scheduled or early or late in the day.
- Multiple groups to be run concurrently
  - First/second-year students who work on campus: Tuesday, March 15, 12:30–2:00 p.m. and Thursday, March 24, 5:00–6:30 p.m.
  - First/second-year students who work off campus: Thursday, March 17, 12:30–2:00 p.m. and Monday, March 29, 5:00–6:30 p.m.
  - Third- and fourth-year students who work on campus: Tuesday, February 15, 3:00–4:30 p.m. and Friday, February 25, 11:00 a.m.–12:30 p.m.

      ○ Third- and fourth- year students who work off campus: Thursday, February 17, 3:00–4:30 p.m. and Monday, February 28, 11:00 a.m.–12:30 p.m.

❖ Who will send the invitation? E-mail or USPS? Will there be an RSVP, and if so, will it be via mail or using a web-based RSVP? Will the groups be first come, first served? Who will contact people a few days before the focus group to confirm their participation (i.e., reminder)?

- Three weeks before each group is conducted, the Office of Assessment will send e-mail invitations to all selected samples with a link to RSVP with screening questions for a group.
- A follow-up confirmation will be sent by the Office of Assessment seven days prior to the scheduled group.
- Phone calls confirming participation will be conducted by the Office of Assessment two days prior to the scheduled group.

❖ Who will greet and welcome the participants?

- Co-moderators

❖ Will there be refreshments served or will a meal be served?

- Lunch (pizza and soda) or afternoon snacks

❖ Will there be incentives? If so, for each participant or one per group based on a random drawing?

- One winner from each group (eight groups) will receive a $100 credit on his or her student ID

❖ What materials will be needed—recorders, tent cards or name tags, markers, newsprint, five-inch-by-eight-inch cards, pens, and so on?

- Two digital recorders per group
- Cardstock for name cards and markers
- Two different color index cards
- Pens

Data Analysis

The focus group team will debrief the moderators within three weeks and then develop the report. The data analysis process includes three stages during which the co-moderators and focus group team review their notes and recordings and have conversations to identify emerging patterns and themes.

- Co-moderators individually review their notes and listen to the recording to produce bulleted themes that are typed into the Moderator's Guide.

- Co-moderators meet to compare and discuss their individual analyses and develop a combined analysis of bulleted themes that are typed into the Moderator's Guide and copied for the focus group team and other co-moderators.
- The focus group team debriefs all the co-moderators in this segment using the Moderator's Guide.
- The focus group team will create the report based on the Moderator's Guide and the information in this proposal.

Time Line

- Moderators will be selected and trained about two weeks prior to the first focus group.
- Focus groups will be conducted in February and March.
- The final report will be submitted to the associate vice president for Enrollment Management by March 31.

Costs

Incentives to participants (mugs, bookmarks, movie tickets)	800
Refreshments/lunch for participants and moderators	2,000
Supplies: markers, five-inch-by-eight-inch cards, newsprint, tent cards/name tags	100
Printing and postage for invitations if mailed	0
Co-moderators ($50/group × 8 groups)	400
Consultants	0
Total	$3,300

Invitation Letter Template

Date

Dear «Title» «Last Name»,

[Briefly identify the topic, the purpose of the focus group project, and why you selected them to participate.]

[Outline the days and time of the groups and if there will be refreshments and remuneration.]

[Tell them what you will do with the information and give people the ability to sign up for a session.]

[Closing thank-you statement.]

Sincerely,

[Signed by a person the population recognizes and will respond to]

Sample Invitation Letters

Project: First-Year Student Success (Accountability)

Segment: First-Year Students

February 27

Dear «First Name»,

We need your help! The university wants to know about your experiences and perceptions of this university and why you decided to return for your second year. This information will help us with programs and services that help students like you.

    I encourage you to tell your story by participating in a focus group on either March 15 from 12:30 to 2:00 p.m. or March 24 from 5:00 to 6:30 p.m. Pizza, soda, and cookies will be served. These focus groups will be confidential.

    Your insight and experiences are extremely important to this effort and will help other students be as successful as you. To sign up for a group, click here.

Kindly,

Curtis Jacobson
President, Student Government Association

Segment: Faculty and Advisers

January 23

Dear «Title» «Last Name»,

We want to learn about your perceptions of the challenges that students face, the resources that they need, and why they decide to stay or leave the institution.

I invite you to participate in a focus group on one of the following days:

- Faculty: Tuesday, February 15, 3:00–4:30 p.m. or Friday, February 25, 8:30–10:00 a.m.
- Advisers: Tuesday, February 8, 8:30–10:00 a.m. or Thursday, February 10, 12:00–1:30 p.m.

These focus groups will be strictly confidential and the results will be reported in aggregate. Breakfast or afternoon snacks will be served.

Your insight and experiences are extremely important to this effort. I greatly appreciate your time and energy and will offer a small token of our appreciation for all participants. To sign up for a group, follow this link: www.samplelink.edu

Sincerely,

Eva Cookman
Provost and Vice President of Academic Affairs

Project: Increasing Underrepresented Student Enrollment (Access)

Segment: First-Year Students

February 27

Dear «First Name»,

We are glad you returned to this university for another semester and now we need your help. We want to know why you decided to attend this university and what has helped you be successful. This information will help us with programs and services that help students like you.

Please come and tell your story by participating in a focus group on either March 15 from 12:30 to 2:00 p.m. or March 24 from 5:00 to 6:30 p.m. Soda, water, cookies, and fruit will be served, and we will also have a small gift to thank you for participating. These focus groups will be confidential.

Your insight and experiences are extremely important to this effort and will help other students be as successful as you. To sign up for a group, click here.

Kindly,

Pamela Pinder
Chair, Diversity Committee
Student Government Association

Segment: Junior Students

February 1

Dear «First Name»,

We are glad you returned to this university for another semester and now we need your help. We want to know why you decided to attend this university and what has helped you be successful. This information will help with programs and services that help students like you.

Please come and tell your story by participating in a focus group on either February 15 from 3:00 to 4:30 p.m. or February 25 from 11:00 a.m. to 12:30 p.m. Soda, water, cookies, and fruit will be served, and we will also have a small gift to thank you for participating. These focus groups will be confidential.

Your insight and experiences are extremely important to this effort and will help other students be as successful as you. To sign up for a group, click here.

Kindly,

Pamela Pinder
Chair, Diversity Committee
Student Government Association

Project: Impact of College Costs and Work on Student Success (Affordability)

Segment: First- and Second-Year Students

February 27

Dear «First Name»,

We need your help with understanding how college costs impact your success. This information will help with programs and services that help students like you.

Please come and tell your story by participating in a focus group on either

- Tuesday, March 15, 12:30–2:00 p.m.
- Thursday, March 17, 12:30–2:00 p.m.
- Thursday, March 24, 5:00–6:30 p.m.
- Monday, March 28, 5:00–6:30 p.m.

Soda, water, cookies, and fruit will be served, and we will also have a small gift to thank you for participating. These focus groups will be confidential.

Your insight and experiences are extremely important to this effort and will help other students be as successful as you. To sign up for a group, click here.

Kindly,

Brian Painter
President
Student Government Association

Segment: Third- and Fourth-Year Students

February 1

Dear «First Name»,

We need your help with understanding how college costs impact your success. This information will help with programs and services that help students like you.

Please come and tell your story by participating in a focus group on either

- Tuesday, February 15, 3:00–4:30 p.m.
- Thursday, February 17, 3:00–4:30 p.m.
- Friday, February 25, 11:00 a.m.–12:30 p.m.
- Monday, February 28, 11:00 a.m.–12:30 p.m.

Soda, water, cookies, and fruit will be served, and we will also have a small gift to thank you for participating. These focus groups will be confidential.

Your insight and experiences are extremely important to this effort and will help other students be as successful as you. To sign up for a group, click here.

Kindly,

Brian Painter
President
Student Government Association

Moderator's Guide Template

I. Introduction (five minutes)
   A. The purpose of this focus group is to_____.
   B. Moderator introductions: "My name is _____ and this is _____. Our job is to facilitate your discussion, record your responses, and keep time to make sure that we thoroughly cover ALL of the topics."
   C. Group Guidelines
      1. Moderators should speak less than one-third of the time.
      2. While one moderator facilitates the discussion the other will be taking notes for analysis, BUT NO NAMES will be recorded.
      3. Respect the confidentiality of each participant by not quoting or attributing comments to anyone outside of the group.
      4. All should participate.
      5. Discussion and disagreement are encouraged; no need to reach consensus.
      6. There are no right or wrong opinions; just different points of view.
      7. Only one person should speak at a time—no side conversations.
      8. Please be open and honest about your attitudes, opinions, and experiences—we want to hear it all.
   D. Audio recording for data analyses
      1. _**ONLY**_ the focus group team will have access to the recordings.
      2. The recordings will be used _**ONLY**_ for data analyses.
      3. _**ONLY**_ group results will be reported and no individuals will be identified; however, we may use some direct quotations to emphasize a particular point.
      4. _**Confidentiality**_: Please keep confidential all information that others share with the group when you leave.
   E. "If there are no questions or concerns, let's begin!"
II. Introduction of participants (10 minutes)
   A. First name and perhaps some other piece of information
III. Warm-up question related to the topic that is completed on a colored index card by each participant

IV. Topic Discussion (60–90 minutes)

A. Topic A
  1.
  2.
  3.
B. Topic B
  1.
  2.
  3.
C. Topic C
  1.
  2.
  3.
D. Topic D
  1.
  2.
  3.
E. Topic E
  1.
  2.
  3.

V. Wrap-up question related to the topic that is completed on a colored index card (different color from the warm-up question) by each participant (10–15 minutes)

THANK YOU!!!

Moderator's Guide Example: First-Year Student Success, Moderator's Guide for Students

I. Introduction (five minutes)

A. The purpose of this focus group is to learn from students why they decide to stay or leave the institution, to obtain student perceptions of the challenges of the undergraduate experience at the institution, and to determine what resources students need to help them be successful.

B. Moderator introductions: "My name is _____ and this is _____. Our job is to facilitate your discussion, record your responses, and keep time to make sure that we thoroughly cover ALL of the topics."

C. Group Guidelines

   1. Moderators should speak less than one-third of the time.

   2. While one moderator facilitates the discussion the other will be taking notes for analysis, BUT NO NAMES will be recorded.

   3. Respect the confidentiality of each participant by not quoting or attributing comments to anyone outside of the group.

   4. All should participate.

   5. Discussion and disagreement are encouraged; no need to reach consensus.

   6. There are no right or wrong opinions; just different points of view.

   7. Only one person should speak at a time—no side conversations.

   8. Please be open and honest about your attitudes, opinions, and experiences—we want to hear it all.

D. Audio recording for data analyses

   1. **_ONLY_** the focus group team will have access to the recordings.

   2. The recordings will be used **_ONLY_** for data analyses.

3. **ONLY** group results will be reported and no individuals will be identified; however, we may use some direct quotations to emphasize a particular point.

4. **Confidentiality**: Please keep confidential all information that others share with the group when you leave.

E. "If there are no questions or concerns, let's begin!"

Contact Information:

Jean Morris, 410-555-2202 (cell)

Jim Watson, 757-555-5218 (cell)

Stephen Calliotte, 955-555-5207 (cell)

II. Introduction of Participants (10 minutes)

    A. First name and major

III. Warm-up question related to the topic **OR** some type of ice-breaker—make sure everyone responds to this item on a PINK index card. Collect cards prior to starting the topic discussion.

What is the most memorable (or surprising) thing about your first year at the university? [Participants write their responses on a card and the co-moderator facilitates a discussion.]

IV. Topic Discussion (60–90 minutes)

    A. Experiences at the university

        1. What are some reasons that you chose to return to the university for a second year?

        2. What are some reasons other students you know did not return?

        3. Please tell us about the quality of your undergraduate experience here.

            a. What about your

                1. academic experiences both in and out of class?

                2. social experiences in the campus community?

    B. Perceptions of Students

        1. What did you find most challenging about your academic experience?

        2. If you were to redo your first semester here, what would you do differently?

    C. Resources Needed to Be Successful

        1. What resources did you use for assistance with academics?

        2. What resources did you use to help you become a member of the university community?

3. What other/additional resources do students need to help them be successful? [If students struggle identifying resources OR if you want to ask about a couple of specific resources, list them here.]

D. Recommendations

1. What recommendations do you have for the incoming class of first-year students?

2. What recommendations do you have for the faculty and administrators who will work with them?

V. Wrap-up (10–15 minutes): Make sure everyone responds to this item on a BLUE index card.

If you had one suggestion for the student success committee, what would it be? [Participants write their responses on a card and the co-moderator facilitates a discussion if there is time. If there is not time for discussion, the co-moderator collects the cards and ends the session.]

THANK YOU!!!

Moderator's Guide Example: First-Year Student Success, Moderator's Guide for Faculty and Advisers

I. Introduction (five minutes)

    A. The purpose of this focus group is to learn why students decide to stay or leave the institution, to obtain faculty and advisers' perceptions of the challenges of the undergraduate experience at the institution, and to determine what resources students need to help them be successful.

    B. Moderator introductions: "My name is _____ and this is _____. Our job is to facilitate your discussion, record your responses, and keep time to make sure that we thoroughly cover ALL of the topics."

    C. Group Guidelines

        1. Moderators should speak less than one-third of the time.

        2. While one moderator facilitates the discussion the other will be taking notes for analysis, BUT NO NAMES will be recorded.

        3. Respect the confidentiality of each participant by not quoting or attributing comments to anyone outside of the group.

        4. All should participate.

        5. Discussion and disagreement are encouraged; no need to reach consensus.

        6. There are no right or wrong opinions; just different points of view.

        7. Only one person should speak at a time—no side conversations.

        8. Please be open and honest about your attitudes, opinions, and experiences—we want to hear it all.

    D. Audio recording for data analyses

        1. _**ONLY**_ the focus group team will have access to the recordings.

        2. The recordings will be used _**ONLY**_ for data analyses.

        3. _**ONLY**_ group results will be reported and no individuals will be identified; however, we may use some direct quotations to emphasize a particular point.

        4. _**Confidentiality**_: Please keep confidential all information that others share with the group when you leave.

E. "If there are no questions or concerns, let's begin!"

Contact Information:
Jean Morris, 410-555-2202 (cell)
Jim Watson, 757-555-5218 (cell)
Stephen Calliotte, 955-555-5207 (cell)

II. Introduction of Participants (10 minutes)
A. First name, department, and role
III. Warm-up question related to the topic—make sure everyone responds to this item on a PINK index card. Collect cards prior to starting the topic discussion.
      What is something unique that you noticed about last year's first-year students? [Participants write their responses on a card and the co-moderator facilitates a discussion.]
IV. Topic Discussion (60–90 minutes)
A. Experiences at the University
1. What is it that you think causes some students to not return to the university for their second year?
2. Why is it that other students choose to return to the university?
3. What are some of the characteristics of our undergraduate experience that help students to be successful
a. academically, both in and out of class?
b. socially in becoming part of the campus community?
B. Perceptions of Students
1. What is it that you think students find most challenging:
a. academically, both in and out of class?
b. socially in becoming part of the campus community?
C. Resources Needed to Be Successful
1. What resources do we offer to students in need of assistance with academics or with becoming a member of the university community?
2. What other/additional resources do students need to help them be successful?
[If faculty and administrators struggle identifying resources OR if you want to ask about a couple of specific resources, list them here.]
D. Recommendations
1. What recommendations do you have for improving the success of the incoming class of first-year students?

V.   Wrap-up (10–15 minutes): Make sure everyone responds to this item on a BLUE index card.

What is one recommendation you would give to first-year students to help them be successful? [Participants write their responses on a card and the co-moderator facilitates a discussion if there is time. If there is not time for discussion, the co-moderator collects the cards and ends the session.]

THANK YOU!!!

Moderator's Guide Example: Increase Underrepresented Student Enrollment

I. Introduction (five minutes)

   A. The purpose of this focus group is to learn about underrepresented students' perceptions of college and the resources they need to be successful.

   B. Moderator introductions: "My name is _____ and this is _____. Our job is to facilitate your discussion, record your responses, and keep time to make sure that we thoroughly cover ALL of the topics."

   C. Group Guidelines

      1. Moderators should speak less than one-third of the time.

      2. While one moderator facilitates the discussion the other will be taking notes for analysis, BUT NO NAMES will be recorded.

      3. Respect the confidentiality of each participant by not quoting or attributing comments to anyone outside of the group.

      4. All should participate.

      5. Discussion and disagreement are encouraged; no need to reach consensus.

      6. There are no right or wrong opinions; just different points of view.

      7. Only one person should speak at a time—no side conversations.

      8. Please be open and honest about your attitudes, opinions, and experiences—we want to hear it all.

   D. Audio recording for data analyses

      1. _**ONLY**_ the focus group team will have access to the recordings.

      2. The recordings will be used _**ONLY**_ for data analyses.

      3. _**ONLY**_ group results will be reported and no individuals will be identified; however, we may use some direct quotations to emphasize a particular point.

      4. _**Confidentiality**_: Please keep confidential all information that others share with the group when you leave.

E. "If there are no questions or concerns, let's begin!"

Contact Information:
Jean Morris, 410-555-2202 (cell)
Jim Watson, 757-555-5218 (cell)
Stephen Calliotte, 955-555-5207 (cell)

II. Introduction of Participants (10 minutes)
   A. First name and major
III. Warm-up question related to the topic—make sure everyone responds to this item on a PINK index card. Collect cards prior to starting the topic discussion.
   When I say **COLLEGE** what is the first thing that comes to mind? [Participants write their responses on a card, and the co-moderator facilitates a discussion.]
IV. Topic Discussion (60–90 minutes)
   A. Attending College
      1. How important was it for you to attend college?
         a. This college?
      2. How important was it for your families that you attended college?
         a. This college?
   B. Deciding to Attend College
      1. What made you decide to attend college?
         a. What made you choose this college?
      2. What worried you about attending college?
         a. This college?
         b. What still worries you?
   C. Student Success
      1. What can this university do to help you be successful?
         a. What can faculty or staff do?
      2. What has helped you be successful during your time here?

V. Wrap-up (10–15 minutes): Make sure everyone responds to this item on a BLUE index card.

> If you had one suggestion for university administrators on how they could help increase underrepresented students' enrollment and success, what would it be? [Participants write their responses on a card and the co-moderator facilitates a discussion if there is time. If there is not time for discussion, the co-moderator collects the cards and ends the session.]

THANK YOU!!!

Moderator's Guide Example: Impact of College Costs and Work on Student Success

I. Introduction (five minutes)

    A. The purpose of this group is to learn about student perspectives on the value of college and the impact costs have on their success.

    B. Moderator introductions: "My name is _____ and this is _____. Our job is to facilitate your discussion, record your responses, and keep time to make sure that we thoroughly cover ALL of the topics."

    C. Group Guidelines

        1. Moderators should speak less than one-third of the time.

        2. While one moderator facilitates the discussion the other will be taking notes for analysis, BUT NO NAMES will be recorded.

        3. Respect the confidentiality of each participant by not quoting or attributing comments to anyone outside of the group.

        4. All should participate.

        5. Discussion and disagreement are encouraged; no need to reach consensus.

        6. There are no right or wrong opinions; just different points of view.

        7. Only one person should speak at a time—no side conversations.

        8. Please be open and honest about your attitudes, opinions, and experiences—we want to hear it all.

    D. Audio recording for data analyses

        1. ***ONLY*** the focus group team will have access to the recordings.

        2. The recordings will be used ***ONLY*** for data analyses.

        3. ***ONLY*** group results will be reported and no individuals will be identified; however, we may use some direct quotations to emphasize a particular point.

        4. ***Confidentiality***: Please keep confidential all information that others share with the group when you leave.

    E. "If there are no questions or concerns, let's begin!"

Contact Information:
Jean Morris, 410-555-2202 (cell)
Jim Watson, 757-555-5218 (cell)
Stephen Calliotte, 955-555-5207 (cell)

II.   Introduction of Participants (10 minutes)
    A.   First name and major
III. Warm-up question related to the topic—make sure everyone responds to this item on a PINK index card. Collect cards prior to starting the topic discussion.

    As you were preparing to come to college for your first year, what most excited you about attending college and what was your greatest concern? [Participants write their responses on a card and the co-moderator facilitates a discussion.]

IV. Topic Discussion (60–90 minutes)
    A.   Value of College
        1.   What is the value of a college education to
            a.   you?
            b.   your family?
        2.   To what extent were college costs (tuition, fees, room and board, books and supplies, etc.) a factor in deciding to attend or remain here?
    B.   Impact of Working on Academic Success
        1.   What is the impact of working [on/off] campus on your academic success?
    C.   Benefit of Working While in College
        1.   What is the benefit of working while attending college, beyond simply earning money?
V.   Wrap-up (10–15 minutes): Make sure everyone responds to this item on a BLUE index card.

If you had one suggestion for students who are working and how they can be successful in college, what would it be? [Participants write their responses on a card, and the co-moderator facilitates a discussion if there is time. If there is not time for discussion, the co-moderator collects the cards and ends the session.]

THANK YOU!!!

Moderator's Training Guide

"The overall mission of a moderator is to elicit inputs from the assembled group that will achieve the objectives of the focus group session established by the researchers" (Greenbaum, 1988, p. 46).

- Moderators "Elicit Inputs"
  - Be alert and free from distractions.
  - Create a friendly, comfortable, inviting atmosphere.
  - Challenge participants to think more critically and deeply about topics.
  - Remain unbiased.
  - LISTEN; be comfortable with silence; talk less than one-third of the time.
  - Attend to your nonverbal behaviors as well as verbal comments.
    - Avoid "that's good" or "excellent."
    - Avoid head nodding as it could be seen as approving the answer.
- Moderators Work With the "Assembled Group"
  - Encourage participants to discuss and disagree.
  - Balance input from introverted and extroverted participants—everyone participates.
    - Use subtle group control by looking away from dominant talkers/ramblers; leverage nonverbal behavior for "shy" participants.
- Moderators "Achieve the Objectives of the Researchers"
  - Be flexible with the Moderator's Guide BUT cover ALL topics in the time allotted.
  - Make connections between comments and conceptual activity.
- Skills to Use During the Group
  - Work with the co-moderator; switch off leading and assisting; assist each other if someone tries to dominate or distract the process.
  - Pauses: Count 5 to 10 seconds after you ask a question, and look around the room for nonverbal behavior.

- o Probes: Dig deeper into an answer:
  - Would you explain further? Tell me more. Could you give an example?
  - What do others think? Have others had similar experiences/thoughts?
  - Avoid "why?"—ask more direct questions about the attitude of the participant or his or her experiences.
  - If a comment is inconsistent with the discussion (current or previous), seek to clarify.
  - o Before moving on to the next question, summarize the discussion, confirm, and ask for other comments.
  - o Take high-level notes during the session and record nonverbals.
- After the Group/Report
  - o DOWNLOAD THE RECORDING and make a second copy.
  - o Summarize themes and key points for each question. These points are typically discussed by several participants.
  - o Include quotes that capture a theme/illustrate a point.
  - o Meet with your co-moderator to compare and contrast themes—merge both moderators' analyses into one report.
- Focus Group Process
  - o Introduction of moderators and process
  - o Introductions of participants and warm-up
  - o Topics (broad, open-ended questions)
  - o Wrap-up (closed question)
- Research Process
  - o Attend training (one hour).
  - o Conduct groups (two hours per group).
  - o Review recordings and identify emerging themes and trends related to each topic; if possible discuss your findings with your co-moderator (two to three hours).
  - o Attend debriefing session (two hours).
- Problems During Focus Groups (Greenbaum, 1988)
  - o Moderator problems—generally the reverse of the characteristics of good moderators
    - Leading rather than guiding
    - Being too knowledgeable
    - Trying to be a comedian/becoming the focus of the group

- Being a poor listener
- Being too rigid with the moderator's guide
- Not relating well to the people in the group
- Being too naïve about the subject of the focus group
- Focusing on individuals rather than the group
- Alienating a group member
  o Facility Problems
- Noise
- Audio/video recording
  o Content Problems
  - Confusing concept
  - Dead subject
  - Lively subject
- Participant Problems
  o Experts and influentials
  o Dominant talkers
  o Disruptive participants
  o Ramblers and wanderers
  o Quiet and shy participants
  o Inattentive participants

Moderator's Thematic Analysis Example: First-Year Student Success, Faculty

NOTE to Reader: As stated in all of the Moderator's Guides and stressed throughout the book, focus group discussions are confidential. Most of the reports we have written are as well. Thus, we conducted an abbreviated mock focus group with colleagues, attempting to do so as realistically as possible. The data analysis follows, and the report appears in Appendix N.

I. Introduction of Participants (10 minutes)
   A. First name, department, and role
      1. Participants came from a wide range of departments (five) across two colleges.
II. Warm-up question related to the topic—make sure everyone responds to this item on a PINK index card. Cards should be collected and briefly discussed prior to starting the topic discussion.
   A. What is something unique that you noticed about last year's (2016) first-year students?
      - "My learning community—their diversity—wide range of backgrounds, skills, abilities, and interests. They varied greatly in their views, which led to interesting discussions—not all wanted to stay."
      - "Difficulty transferring from high school expectations to college expectations—in terms of responsibility to work without constant checks, homework, etc."
      - "—very by the book
         —need a lot of attention
         —political affected some of their climate
         —participation—first-time voters"
      - "Most of them like technology, like cell phones, computers, etc. I can use that to my advantage. . . ."
      - "The first-year students who came in during the 2016–17 year seemed more equipped for project-based learning than other cohorts; perhaps this is due to the uptick in specialized K–12 schools in the area in the last few years."
      - "They seem to be quite outgoing and very socially engaged, whether with peers or with the greater campus community."

CARD and DISCUSSION THEMES

First-year students still need assistance with transition into college, but seem more apt to participate in classroom activities and more socially engaged in the campus community.

   III. Topic Discussion (60–90 minutes)
      A. Experiences at the university
         1. What is it that you think causes some students to not return to the university for their second year?

THEMES

- Connections/sense of belonging to university
  - Students need to understand why they are here (at an institution) and connect how their work in the classroom connects with their learning.
  - When these connections are not made, their academics may suffer and they will likely end up in debt.
- Connections/sense of belonging to faculty
  - Students need to make a connection to faculty so they have someone to go to when they need help or to ask questions.
  - Faculty need to take time to understand how to make connections with students, whether that be knowing their first names or using examples that are relevant to their world.
- Connections/sense of belonging to faculty
  - Students need to make connections with other students for help with courses and navigating the institution.
- Maturity
  - We may be asking students to mature too fast. They are not adults, but we treat them as if they are on their own. They do not possess the academic skills to be responsible for their own learning yet.
  - First-generation students may not understand what it takes to be successful in college or whom to ask. Their families are less knowledgeable and cannot offer the support students need. Furthermore, families of first-generation students do not understand the stress the student may be under and can cause more stress if they do not know when to support, push, or "back off."

2. Why is it that some students choose to return to the university?

THEMES

- Engaging classroom learning experiences
  - o Faculty are engaging in and out of the classroom with students, whether that be adjusting their teaching styles, creating opportunities in class to connect and get to know students better, or linking knowledge to real-world experiences through learning communities or service-learning projects.
- Students need information relevant to their present situation or experience.
  - o "Firehose approach to orientation"—we give students information about their entire college career in the summer orientation, when they really need to know only day-to-day steps to help them be successful (i.e., going to class). Practices that give students relevant information on how to be successful are more likely to help students digest information when they need it and understand the steps they need to take.

3. What are some of the characteristics of our undergraduate experience that helps students to be successful:
   a. Academically, both in and out of class?

THEMES

- Practices that connect students to resources and peers for help and support allow students to find information when they need it from multiple people (e.g., early alert grades, peer mentoring).

   b. Socially in becoming part of the campus community?

THEMES

- This is difficult for academics/faculty to discuss, so we tend to yield to student affairs professionals for help with connecting what is learned/taught inside the classroom to outside activities (e.g., cocurricular).

- Students who create social connections with other students in their classes tend to be more engaged in on-campus activities and classes.

IV. Wrap-up (10–15 minutes): Make sure everyone responds to this item on a BLUE index card.

A. What is one recommendation you would give to first-year students to help them be successful?

- "Come from a place of yes—
  —say yes to invitations from professors to events on campus
  —say yes to study groups
  —say yes to at least one student organization
  —say yes to Activity Hour events
  —say yes to office hours."
- "I would recommend them to seek help constantly. There is nothing wrong with being helped. Also that it is okay to fail. Failure is not the problem, the problem is not to stand up again and continue trying."
- "Go to class and talk to your faculty member—they are here to help you. Find something that is fun—academic, social, etc. Be willing to get outside your comfort zone."
- "Find a mentor and ask for help! (Your professors are desperate to lend a hand to those who are really trying to figure this college thing out. So go to office hours and tell them what's happening in and out of the classroom. Their every dream is to find a way to make each student successful.)"
- "To be successful go to every class and be engaged with the learning process—own it and measure your value by what you learn—not your grade."
- "Don't be afraid to ask question(s) about anything in any situation! Everybody is here to help you to be successful."

CARD THEMES

- Everyone on campus is here to help; make connections with faculty and students and ask questions constantly.

Final Report Example: First-Year Student Success, Faculty Focus Group Report

NOTE to Reader: Our intention with this sample report is to provide the reader with an example of what a finished thematic analysis of focus group data resembles. It should be noted that the summary in this report is based on one shortened focus group; therefore, it is not as robust as a full report would be, and the summary is sparse.

In February 2017, two focus groups were conducted to solicit feedback from faculty about first-year (FY) student success. Specifically, student affairs wanted to know:

- What factors influence FY students' decision to stay at an institution?
- What are FY students' perceptions of their experiences?
- What factors contributed to FY students' success?

Faculty were asked a series of questions related to FY students' experiences at the institution, their perceptions of FY students, the resources students may need, and recommendations on how to help FY students be successful in college. The specific questions asked are listed at the end of this report.

Faculty who teach FY undergraduate courses were randomly selected and invited to participate in one of the two groups. There were a total of 16 faculty members (8 per group), from 9 different departments, across 3 colleges that participated. Two co-moderators (administrative faculty and tenured faculty) facilitated each 90-minute group. The moderators were trained and used a common Moderator's Guide. Thematic analyses were conducted on the information collected from the groups. The data presented represent a combined summary of the groups.

Summary

Themes

There were some overarching themes across all the questions asked. Faculty participants noted the importance of connections—to learning, faculty, and other students. Without these connections, FY students may not be successful and opt to leave college.

Connection to Learning
Faculty noted that students who are able to connect what they have learned in the classroom to their own current experiences or potential future work experiences tend to have more success in college. Those who do not make those connections and cannot answer why they are in college tend to disengage from academic and social interactions. This disengagement leads to academic and possible financial troubles that lead to a decision to leave an institution.

Connection to Faculty
Most faculty discussed the importance of students connecting with their faculty. Without this connection, it can be difficult for faculty to know when a student needs help and the types of resources to provide. Participants recognized the role faculty can play in helping FY students be successful.

Connection to Peers
Social connections to peers was another theme that emerged during the focus group discussions. Faculty noted that they have difficulty with out-of-the-class activities and defer to student affairs professionals. Faculty recognized that students who are engaged in cocurricular activities that connect classroom learning to out-of-the class-experience seem to be more successful. Additionally, those who connect to peers tend to be more engaged in on-campus activities.

Recommendations

Faculty agreed that students need help with academic and social engagement. Once engaged, FY students seem to be more successful than those who are not. Furthermore, faculty are willing to help students connect to resources, but they need to know when the student needs help.

Because connections to learning and peers occur within and outside of the classroom, faculty need help from student support services and other professionals to ensure students have access to the help and support they need. With this partnership, FY students can find connections across the institutions that will help them learn and persist.

FY Student Success Focus Groups Moderator's Guide

    I. Introduction of Participants (10 minutes)
        A. First name, department, and role

    II. Ask a warm-up question related to the topic **_OR_** some type of icebreaker—make sure **everyone** responds to this item on a PINK index card. Collect cards prior to starting the topic discussion.

        What is something unique that you noticed about last year's FY students? [Participants write their responses on a card and the co-moderator facilitates a discussion.]

    III. Topic Discussion (60–90 minutes)
        A. Experiences at the University
- What is it that you think causes some students to not return to the university for their second year?
- Why is it that other students choose to return to the university?
- What are some of the characteristics of our undergraduate experience that helps students to be successful
  - academically, both in and out of class?
  - socially in becoming part of the campus community?

        B. Perceptions of Students
- What is it that you think students find most challenging:
  - academically, both in and out of class?
  - socially in becoming part of the campus community?

        C. Resources Needed to Be Successful
- What resources do we offer to students in need of assistance with academics or with becoming a member of the university community?
- What other/additional resources do students need to help them be successful?

        [If faculty and administrators struggle identifying resources OR if you want to ask about a couple of specific resources, list them here.]

D. Recommendations
- What recommendations do you have for improving the success of the incoming class of FY students?

IV. Wrap-up (10–15 minutes): Make sure everyone responds to this item on a BLUE index card.

What is one recommendation you would give to first-year students to help them be successful? [Participants write their responses on a card and the co-moderator facilitates a discussion if there is time. If there is not time for discussion, the co-moderator collects the cards and ends the session.]

Logistics Checklist

Dates
      Times

Location
      Room
      Conference table
      Refreshments table
      Nine to 12 chairs
      Restrooms nearby
      Accessible

Refreshments
      To eat
      To drink
      Catering order

Incentives per participant

Gifts, one per group or several groups

Invitations

RSVPs

Supplies per group (in bag, box, or basket)
    Two digital recorders
      Extra batteries
    Pens per participant
    Tent cards per participant (for names)
    Markers (for tent cards)
    Five-inch-by-eight-inch cards per participant in two different colors
      (warm-up and wrap-up questions)
    Expanded Moderator's Guides per moderator
    Organizer or Research Team contact information

Arum, R., & Roksa, J. (2010). *Academically adrift: Limited learning on college campuses.* Chicago, IL: The University of Chicago Press.

Arum, R., & Roksa, J. (2011, January 18). Are undergraduates actually learning anything? *The Chronicle of Higher Education.* Retrieved from http://chronicle.com/article/Are-Undergraduates-Actually/125979

Belkin, D., & Thurm, S. (2012, December 28). Deans list: Hiring spree fattens college bureaucracy—and tuition. *Wall Street Journal.* Retrieved from http://online.wsj.com/news/articles/SB100014241278873233168045781614907160 42814

Black, J., & Champion, D. (1976). *Methods and issues in social research.* New York, NY: Wiley.

Boyce, C., & Neale, P. (2006). *Conducting in-depth interviews: A guide for designing and conducting in-depth interviews for evaluation input.* Watertown, MA: Pathfinder International.

Bureau of Labor Statistics. (2016). *Earnings and unemployment rates by educational attainment, 2015.* Retrieved from http://www.bls.gov/emp/ep_chart_001.htm

Cameron, W. (1963). *Informal sociology: A casual introduction to sociological thinking.* New York, NY: Random House.

Conner, T. W., & Rabovsky, T. M. (2011). Accountability, affordability, access: A review of the recent trends in higher education policy research. *Policy Studies Journal, 39,* 93–112.

Constable, P., & Clement, S. (2014, January 31). Hispanics often lead the way in their faith in the American dream, poll finds. *Washington Post.* Retrieved from http://www.washingtonpost.com/local/hispanics-often-lead-the-way-in-their-faith-in-the-american-dream-poll-finds/2014/01/30/c9d4d498-6c2a-11e3-b405-7e360f7e9fd2_story.html

Creswell, J. W. (2014). *Research design: Qualitative, quantitative, and mixed methods approaches* (4th ed.). Los Angeles, CA: Sage.

Cutler, D. M., & Lleras-Muney, A. (2012). *Education and health: Insights from international comparisons.* National Bureau of Economic Research. Retrieved from http://www.nber.org/papers/w17738

Eagan, K., Stolzenberg, E. B., Bates, A. K., Aragon, M. C., Suchard, M. R., & Rose-Aguilar, C. (2016). *The American freshman: National norms fall 2015.* Los Angeles, CA: Higher Education Research Institute.

Egerter, S., Braveman, P., Sadegh-Nobari, T., Grossman-Kahn, R., & Dekker, M. (2009). *Education matters for health.* San Francisco, CA: Robert Wood Johnson Foundation Commission to Build a Healthier America.

Given, L. (Ed.). (2008). *The SAGE encyclopedia of qualitative research methods.* Los Angeles, CA: Sage.

Greenbaum, T. L. (1988). *The practical handbook and guide to focus group research.* Lexington, MA: Lexington Books.

Gubrium, J., & Holstein, J. (2001). *Handbook of interview research.* Los Angeles, CA: Sage.

Hadley, R. G., & Mitchell, L. K. (1995). *Counseling research and program evaluation.* Pacific Grove, CA: Brooks/Cole.

Hannah-Jonessept, N. (2015, September 9). A prescription for more black doctors. *New York Times.* Retrieved from https://www.nytimes.com/2015/09/13/magazine/a-prescription-for-more-black-doctors.html

Hart Research Associates. (2013). *It takes more than a major: Employer priorities for college learning and student success.* Washington, DC: Hart Research Associates. Retrieved from https://www.aacu.org/sites/default/files/files/LEAP/2013_EmployerSurvey.pdf

Immerwahr, J., & Johnson, J. (2010). *Squeeze play 2010: Continued public anxiety on cost, harsher judgments on how colleges are run.* New York, NY: Public Agenda. Retrieved from http://www.publicagenda.org/files/SqueezePlay2010report.pdf

Jaschik, S. (2011, January 18). Academically adrift. *Inside Higher Ed.* Retrieved from https://www.insidehighered.com/news/2011/01/18/study_finds_large_numbers_of_college_students_don_t_learn_much

Jaschik, S. (2012, February 27). Santorum's attacks on higher ed. *Inside Higher Ed.* Retrieved from http://www.insidehighered.com/news/2012/02/27/santorums-views-higher-education-and-satan#ixzz37YRiKwZB

Johnson, B., & Christensen, L. (2004). *Educational research: Quantitative, qualitative and mixed approaches* (2nd ed.). Boston, MA: Pearson Education.

Julian, T. A. (2012). *Work-life earnings by field of degree and occupation for people with a bachelor's degree: 2011.* American Community Survey Briefs, ACSBR/11-04. Washington, DC: U.S. Census Bureau. Retrieved from http://www.census.gov/prod/2012pubs/acsbr11-04.pdf

Julian, T. A., & Kominski, R. A. (2011). *Education and synthetic work-life earnings estimates.* American Community Survey Reports, ACS-14. Washington, DC: U.S. Census Bureau. Retrieved from http://www.census.gov/prod/2011pubs/acs-14.pdf

Keierleber, M. (2014, April 10). 15 papers on college affordability are released at Lumina event. *The Chronicle of Higher Education.* Retrieved from http://www.chronicle.com/article/15-Papers-on-College/145917

Kiley, K. (2013, January 30). Another liberal arts critic. *Inside Higher Ed.* Retrieved from http://www.insidehighered.com/news/2013/01/30/north-carolina-governor-joins-chorus-republicans-critical-liberal-arts#ixzz37YTGv76z

Krueger, R. A. (1998). *Moderating focus groups: Focus group kit 4.* Thousand Oaks, CA: Sage.

Krueger, R. A., & Casey, M. A. (2015). *Focus groups: A practical guide for applied research* (5th ed.). Thousand Oaks, CA: Sage.

Kvale, S., & Brinkmann, S. (2009). *Interviews: Learning the craft of qualitative research interviewing.* Los Angeles, CA: Sage.

Martin, A. (2012, December 13). Building a showcase campus, using an I.O.U. *New York Times*. Retrieved from http://www.nytimes.com/2012/12/14/business/colleges-debt-falls-on-students-after-construction-binges.html

Mitchell, M., & Leachman, M. (2015). *Years of cuts threaten to put college out of reach for more students*. Washington, DC: Center on Budget and Policy Priorities. Retrieved from http://www.cbpp.org/sites/default/files/atoms/files/5-13-15sfp.pdf

Moore, J., & Rago, M. (2007). *The working student's experience: The hidden costs of working on college student success, engagement, and retention*. National Survey of Student Engagement. Retrieved from http://nsse.indiana.edu/pdf/conference_presentations/2007/The_Working_Students_Experience.pdf

Morgan, D. L. (1988). *Focus groups as qualitative research*. Newbury Park, CA: Sage.

Morgan, D. L. (1997). *Focus groups as qualitative research* (2nd ed.). Thousand Oaks, CA: Sage.

Morgan, D. L., & Scannell, A. U. (1998). *Planning focus groups*. Thousand Oaks, CA: Sage.

National Center for Education Statistics. (2012). *The condition of education 2013*. Washington, DC. Retrieved from https://nces.ed.gov/programs/coe/pdf/Indicator_CVA/COE_CVA_2013_05.pdf

National Center for Education Statistics. (2015). *The condition of education 2015*. Washington, DC. Retrieved from https://nces.ed.gov/pubs2015/2015144.pdf

National Center for Education Statistics. (2017). *The condition of education 2017*. Washington, DC. Retrieved from https://nces.ed.gov/pubs2017/2017144.pdf

Parker, R. (1993). Threats to the validity of research. *Rehabilitation Counseling Bulletin, 36*(3), 131–138.

Pew Research Center. (2014, February). *The rising cost of not going to college*. Retrieved from http://www.pewsocialtrends.org/2014/02/11/the-rising-cost-of-not-going-to-college/

Rawlings, H. R., III. (2014, July 9). Texas makes an appalling mess of education "reform." *The Chronicle of Higher Education*. Retrieved from http://www.chronicle.com/article/Texas-Makes-an-Appalling-Mess/147561/

Seidman, I. (2013). *Interviewing as qualitative research: A guide for researchers in education and social sciences* (4th ed.). New York, NY: Teachers College Press.

Shadish, W., Cook, T., & Campbell, D. (2002). *Experimental and quasi-experimental designs for generalized causal inference*. Boston, MA: Houghton Mifflin.

The 13 most useless majors from philosophy to journalism. (2012, April 23). *Daily Beast*. Retrieved from http://www.thedailybeast.com/galleries/2012/04/23/the-13-most-useless-majors-from-philosophy-to-journalism.html

U.S. Census Bureau. (2013, September 13). *After a recent upswing, college enrollment declines, Census Bureau reports*. Retrieved from https://www.census.gov/newsroom/press-releases/2013/cb13-153.html

U.S. Census Bureau. (2016). *Educational attainment in the United States: 2015*. Retrieved from http://www.census.gov/hhes/socdemo/education/data/cps/historical/fig2.jpg

sound has become a high priority for accrediting agencies and therefore also for higher education institutions. Bringing together the higher education assessment literature with the psychometric literature, this book focuses on how to practice sound assessment.

22883 Quicksilver Drive
Sterling, VA 20166-2019   Subscribe to our e-mail alerts: www.Styluspub.com

Measuring Noncognitive Variables brings together theory, research, and practice related to noncognitive variables in a practical way by using assessment methods provided at no cost. Noncognitive variables have been shown to correlate with the academic success of students of all races, cultures, and backgrounds.

The Analytics Revolution in Higher Education

Edited by Jonathan S. Gagliardi, Amelia Parnell, and Julia Carpenter-Hubin

Foreword by Randy L. Swing

In this era of "Big Data," institutions of higher education are challenged to make the most of the information they have to improve student learning outcomes, close equity gaps, keep costs down, and address the economic needs of the communities they serve at the local, regional, and national levels. This book helps readers understand and respond to this "analytics revolution," examining the evolving dynamics of the institutional research function and the many audiences that institutional researchers need to serve.

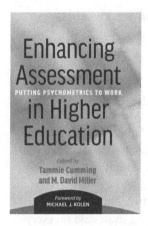

Enhancing Assessment in Higher Education

Edited by Tammie Cumming and M. David Miller

Foreword by Michael J. Kolen

"Enhancing Assessment in Higher Education is a valuable addition to assessment practitioners' bookshelves, especially for those who want a deeper understanding of the vocabulary and methods for evaluating the validity and reliability of their assessments of student learning."

—**Linda Suskie**, *Assessment and Accreditation Consultant*

Assessment and accountability are now inescapable features of the landscape of higher education, and ensuring that these assessments are psychometrically

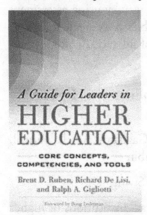

A Guide for Leaders in Higher Education

Core Concepts, Competencies, and Tools

Brent D. Ruben, Richard De Lisi and
Ralph A. Gigliotti

Foreword by Doug Lederman

At a time when higher education faces the unprecedented challenges of declining revenues and increased scrutiny, there is an urgent need for leadership that is conversant with, and able to deploy, the competencies, management tools, and strategic skills that go beyond the technical or disciplinary preparation and "on the job" training that most leaders have received.

Intended as a practical resource for academic and administrative leaders in higher education who seek guidance in dealing with today's complexity, opportunities, and demands, this book is also addressed to those who aspire to hold positions of leadership, and to the many faculty and staff members who serve in informal leadership roles. Additionally, the book serves as a guide and resource for those responsible for the design and implementation of leadership development programs in higher education.

Measuring Noncognitive Variables

Improving Admissions, Success, and Retention for Underrepresented Students

William Sedlacek

Foreword by David Kalsbeek

"William Sedlacek, the 'father of noncognitive variables' in higher education, has impacted millions of college students around the world. With over 40 years of research, his new book reveals the importance of noncognitive skill measurement and development. This is a must-read for every institution and individual genuinely interested in strategically engaging and retaining diverse groups."

—**Connie Tingson-Gatuz**, *PhD, Vice President for Student Affairs and Michigan Integration Madonna University*

(Continued on preceding page)